SCALE MODEL
TUGS &
TRAWLERS

SCALE MODEL
TUGS &
TRAWLERS
Tom Gorman

Nexus Special Interests

Scale Model Tugs and Trawlers

Nexus Special Interests Ltd.
Nexus House
Azalea Drive
Swanley
Kent BR8 8HU

First published 1999

ISBN 1-85486-188-3

Printed and bound in Great Britain by Bookcraft (Bath) Ltd

Contents

Acknowledgements

It is really not possible to produce a book of this nature without the help and assistance of others, some of whom provide support during the work, by reading and commenting upon the work as it proceeds and others who give so freely of their time and effort in providing data. I must, therefore, pass my sincere thanks to the following without whose help I am sure this work would be but a dream.

To John Noble of the Onward Fishing Company who provided very nearly all the data I needed on the fishing boats and who has been a source of help for a number of years.

To my colleague and partner John Orriss, to David Holland who has done the correcting work on the text of this book and to Peter Chappell - mainly for his ribald comments at frequent intervals.

To John Bowen for the input given so generously over the years and others too numerous to mention.

To Yvonne and Margaret who I dare not omit here for they look after me and my needs so well.

The friendliness of the fishing fraternity at the ports of Grimsby, Whitby and others is noteworthy and rarely have I ever been met with blank refusal to answer my never-ending questions. It is impossible to list all those who have helped with data, photographs etc., but I thank them all for their help and assistance.

The kit manufacturers mentioned have also provided a great deal of help for both sections of the book and I hope that they will continue to produce ever better kits for the model shipbuilder. Although there are only few shipbuilders left in the UK I must thank those too who have helped with information and drawings.

Introduction

The information provided in this book comes from a variety of sources: my own experiences on Tyneside watching and sailing with many different vessels, data gleaned from reading and researching for many models, and the invaluable information found within the covers of British Steam Tugs by P N Thomas (Waine Research Publications), which must surely be the model tug master's manual.

This book is written to provide information and data for those who wish to build and sail model tugs and powered fishing vessels as distinct from other types of craft. There is a growing interest in working ships at the present time but an increasing lack of information as shipyards close and building work is carried out in foreign yards. From many years of experience, and with the invaluable assistance of a number of expert friends and fellow modellers, the following chapters will guide the model shipbuilder through the realms of the tug and fishing vessel.

To give the fullest possible guidance to the model builder the book is divided into three sections:

Section One - Tugs, detailing the development of the tug from the early steam-driven ships to the present day

Section Two - Trawlers, detailing the development of the powered fishing vessel from the early days of steam to the present day.

Section Three - Modelling notes, detailing painting and finishing the model, tools and other data to aid the model building process.

Today there is a range of kits available to assist the prospective modeller in building a fine scale model ship, and within this range of kits are a number covering the subjects of this volume. Details of many of these kits are given in the following chapters and to provide help to the newcomer to the hobby a full photographic and written description of building up a kit for a tug is given through the chapters of Section One. In a similar manner the building of a fishing boat from raw materials and drawings is detailed through Section Two.

The initial chapters in each section provide introductory information leading to more detailed data in the later chapters. Development of the ships described in each section is fully

Model of Thames steam tug built from an early Marvon Models kit.

American harbour tug Akron *built of wood to a scale of 1:32.*

Wyeforce - *a model harbour and ship handling tug built from a Model Slipway kit (photo courtesy Model Slipway).*

Irishman - *a model salvage tug built from a Model Slipway kit (photo courtesy Model Slipway).*

covered from the earliest steam-driven craft to the latest and most sophisticated vessels. To assist the modeller also there are chapters dealing with model motive power - applicable to either section - and covering electric and steam-driven equipment. Within the limits of a book of this size it is not possible to give finite data on the sizing of some drive equipment but good sensible guidance is given where possible. Hints and tips on the use of materials and adhesives are included together with advice on painting and finishing the model ship.

There is information provided in both sections regarding the selection and fitting of radio control equipment together with information on fitting the chosen model with auxiliary features of various kinds. Many modellers will wish to enter their models into one or more of the competitions or regattas held throughout the summer at many model boat clubs. Tug-towing competitions are popular, as are steering regattas where model ships are sailed through a set course to gain points for accuracy. Some of the regattas also have sections in which the models are judged for accuracy and quality off the water.

Information on how to prepare models for such competitions is given together with advice on how the full-size ship would have been sailed. In the later chapters will be found details of the various organisations devoted to model ships and of the national competitions for ship models. The benefits of joining a model club and how membership can be of value are also explored.

Chapter 1   Tugs in general

The tug first appeared in the early part of the nineteenth century following the development of the steam engine. Initially they were designed specifically to pull the large sailing ships out from the ports to the open sea and vice versa, but they also served the fishing fleets in many ways. Quite often a steam tug would be used to meet the fishing fleet and to receive the catch for speedy transport to the fish docks when the sailing smacks would take a day or more longer due to adverse winds etc. The manoeuvring of a large ship in shallow water is extremely difficult and often it is very difficult to maintain steerage way in narrow confined waterways - here tugs are used to move the larger vessels. Regretfully, with the advent of bow and stern thrusters and other aids, the large ships of today have little need for tugs and, of course, a ship that can safely berth without the assistance of tugs saves the cost of the tugs and their crews. It all comes down to money in the end.

Tugs can be divided into roughly four categories as follows:

Harbour tugs - generally small ships designed to operate within the confines of the harbour or river in which they worked. Little more than a large engine surrounded by a ship's shell, it had as deep a draft as could be accommodated in the waters of the location - deep draft at the stern being essential to allow the propeller(s) to exert maximum thrust.

The tow hook was usually attached to a suitably strengthened part of the after superstructure and the accommodation was basic, allowing only for daily use without sleeping berths. Usually each tug carried a small boat, and the engine room skylights and other parts of the aft accommodation were protected by towing bows to guide the ropes freely.

River tugs - these were not quite so restricted as the harbour tugs but in many rivers they also had to enter the confines of docks where restrictions required that they too had to be designed to suit the area in which they worked. Frequently such tugs would be required to handle barges, both laden and unladen, and also to tow hoppers of spoil, dredged from the river channels, out to dumping grounds offshore. They were thus built with more sheer and were beamier than the harbour tug in order to withstand the weather and rigours of the open sea. The outfit of these tugs included the same equipment as the harbour tug, supplemented often by radar and fire monitors so that they could assist in handling fires on board ships.

Coastal tugs - were generally larger and suitable for doing coastal towing when there was insufficient work in the river or harbour from which they normally operated. The accommodation included cabin berths for the crew and officers as they often worked away for periods of some days. Their powerful engines gave them a reasonable turn of speed so that they could answer distress calls - 15 to 18 knots was not unusual. As with the smaller tugs they had tow hooks attached to the aft superstructure and frequently had two sizes of hook to allow for differing tows. Two lifeboats in davits were usual and often a small workboat would be carried beneath the towing bows on the stern deck. The radio, radar and sounding equipment was usually as sophisticated as cost would allow.

Ocean-going tugs - are much larger than the previous types. They are designed for long ocean voyages and for salvage work and have a fairly high free-running speed to allow them to attend a ship in distress quickly. They usually carry a range of equipment such as compressors, pumps and generators etc., to service a ship where there may be total engine-room failure, flooding or other damage. The accommodation is generous and most have air conditioning and enclosed superstructures to allow crews to work comfortably in all weathers and areas, varying from the Tropics to the Arctic. They carry large lifeboats and use an automatic winch system in preference to a hook for towing. One or more heavy lift derricks or cranes are fitted to handle the equipment and the towing beams over the aft deck are high enough to permit crew members to walk beneath.

There were, and are, other tugs which do not fall into the above categories such as the Thames lighterage tugs built and used almost exclusively for moving barges. There is also the tug tender used, not only for towing, but for transporting passengers and luggage to large liners lying at anchor offshore or in the deep water of an estuary or river. The latter make excellent and unusual models but at the time of writing there are no kits produced for this type of ship - the prospective builder will have to work from drawings and build a hull in the plank-on-frame or bread-and-butter fashion as described in Section Two.

In the early days the first tugs were paddle-driven with quite crude engines and boilers. Development of the steam engine and boiler, together with the feathering paddle wheel, soon brought the paddle tug into extensive use and, in fact, paddle tugs were in use by the Admiralty into the 1960s. Drawings of many paddle tugs can be found in the libraries of most plans services. Kingston Mouldings (see Appendix 1) offer a hull of grp (glass-reinforced plastic) and drawings of a Director class paddle tug which was launched in 1956 for Admiralty service. To date, however, only the German kit-making firm of Graupner offers a paddle tug model whose *Glasgow* paddle tug includes beautifully made, fully feathering paddles and to a scale of 1:32. The paddle sets are

available as separate kits to those who wish to build a different pattern tug.

Paddle tugs did have independent paddle control and were capable of turning within their own length, but in model form it is much wiser to link the paddles together and drive them from a single power source. Running one paddle full ahead and one full astern can very quickly cause the model to capsize, with the additional problem that when paddles are each being driven separately there is a tendency for the model tug to waddle like a duck as it is almost impossible to obtain two motors that have identical speeds at the same throttle setting. Details of feathering paddles are shown in the accompanying sketch. They require care when making but are not outside the capabilities of the average modeller.

Kits for building screw-driven tugs are available from a number of manufacturers both in the UK and overseas. A list of such kit makers is given in Appendix 1 and illustrations of some of their models are also provided in the following chapters. As with all commercially produced equipment there is a wide variance in what is included with the kit, and it is incumbent upon the modeller to ensure that he/she realises the shortcomings and provides for any additional parts and materials needed. In general a full kit, when bought, will contain all the materials and parts that the modeller requires except for adhesives and paint. Rarely will the kit contain drive equipment or radio control gear and the cost of such equipment will need to be found and added to the kit costs.

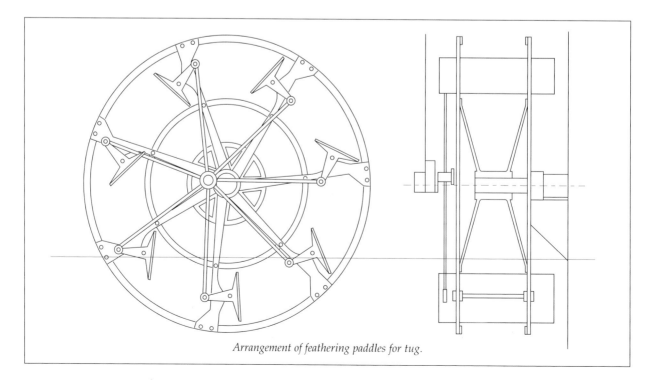

Arrangement of feathering paddles for tug.

Steam paddle tug Glasgow *from a Graupner kit* (photo courtesy Graupner).

A number of manufacturers offer what are commonly called 'semi-kits' which are available in separate lots. Grp hulls with drawings can be bought from some sources (see Appendix 1) and some makers offer packs of fittings that can be bought as and when they are needed, thus spreading the cost of making the model over the construction period. This is also a way of building the model of your choice when a full kit is not available, but it is best to start with a simple kit if you have not had previous experience of model ship-building. Most makers of full kits have one or more simple kits in their range which will allow the newcomer to ship modelling to build and get a model on the water quickly and generally these are not expensive. The bigger and more complex kits, and the building of models from raw materials or from hull and drawing sets, can be tackled when some experience has been gained.

The development of certain types of propulsion, such as the bow and stern thrusters fitted to larger ships which have contributed so much to the decline of the tug, have also had an effect upon the propulsion of the tug. Many modern tugs are now fitted with sophisticated drive equipment,

including Schottel and Voith Schneider systems, which permit easy turning and rapid movement in all directions from control upon the bridge and in the hands of the tug master. Diesel engines too have been developed to provide more power from smaller units, and all have added to make the tug a better unit with service geared to alternative work rather than just the simple towing that was required in the earlier days.

Through the ensuing chapters you will find that it is not necessary to have a workshop packed with sophisticated and expensive tools as it is quite possible to build fine working models with a few good quality tools. It is very wise, however, to buy the very best tools that you can afford as cheap tools very rarely do the job for which they are intended and quite often they fail very quickly. Note that it is not the sharp, keen tool that slips and cuts the user but the blunt tool that needs much too much pressure to effect the cut.

Building from a kit requires fewer tools than building from raw materials (scratch): a good sharp craft knife (preferably of the snap-off blade type); a steel rule; a cutting mat to avoid losing blade points; a small drill with a selection of bits; a selection of small files; a glasspaper block and a selection of differing grades of glasspaper will probably be sufficient to start the work. Those kits which contain timber and plywood parts will show the need for a small handsaw or fretsaw, but fine plywood can be successfully cut with a sharp craft knife and a steel rule. The rule should, for preference, be marked with both imperial and metric measurements and a stainless steel 12-inch rule is ideal for modelling work.

Many of the modern ship kits make extensive use of styrene sheet (plastic or plasticard as it is sometimes called) and the sheets are often printed with the outlines and details of the section of the kit referred to. This material is clean and easy to use - it is simply cut by scoring along the cutting line after which it can be snapped apart. The scoring raises a bead along the edges of the sheet which needs to be removed by sanding or scraping with the edge of the knife before being joined to neighbouring parts.

Joining styrene parts together is best done using liquid polystyrene cement and a small fine brush. The parts to be joined should be held together lightly, the brush charged with liquid polystyrene cement should be drawn along the joint and the joint held for a minute or two. The liquid welds the parts together by chemical action and the pieces can be handled after a few minutes. However, the joint will not be fully cured for at

Neptune - *model of a small harbour tug from a Robbe kit. This is ideal for beginners* (photo courtesy Robbe Schluter UK).

least 12 hours and sanding or cleaning for painting should be not be done too soon after the joints are effected. Adhesives for joining timber to timber abound, but for a waterproof joint that will withstand immersion in water the best is Cascamite which comes in powder form to be mixed with clean water to a thick cream for use. It is a resin glue which has a very slow cure time so that parts joined with Cascamite will need to be held or clamped together for some hours to allow the glue to cure. A quicker grabbing adhesive for timber, but not quite so impervious to water

An American harbour tug model, Akron.

Detail of deck beams and support triangles on the hull of the model tug Cruiser.

immersion, is PVA (polyvinyl acetate) of the aliphatic type. This is a resin glue of creamy white appearance which dries hard to a transparent finish and has a grab time of only a few minutes. Parts can actually be hand-held until the glue sets enough for safe handling but, again, the full cure of the adhesive is not reached for some 12 hours after use and, in the same way as for the polystyrene cement, the joints need to be left for some hours before they are sanded and prepared for painting or other work.

For joining unlike materials such as styrene sheet to timber, surfaces should be roughened first to provide a key for the adhesive and cyanoacrylate (superglue) is probably best although one of the two-part epoxy cements may suffice. For metal to timber and styrene, superglue is also a good method. For joining timber or styrene to grp then the best adhesive is catalysed polyester resin, but

two-part epoxy of the slow cure type will do. Details of these adhesives are given in appropriate places throughout the following chapters.

The kit *Cruiser* - introduction

As previously explained, there are different types of tugs and it is not possible to describe the building of each type. The similarities of one type to another will become apparent when the accompanying photographs are studied. The following description of building a model tug from a kit is therefore offered to assist the modeller. The kit is of the steam tug *Cruiser* produced by Mount Fleet Models (see Appendix 1 for details), a single screw coastal tug, the prototype for which was originally built by Hall Russell & Co. of Aberdeen in 1953. She was one of the last coal-fired steam tugs to be built (for the Glasgow tug owners, Steel & Bennie). A very full description

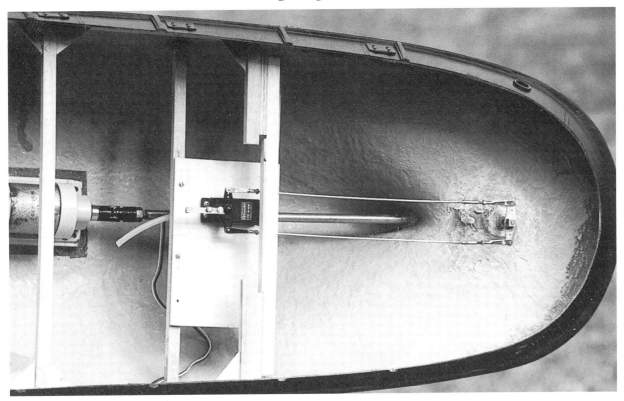

Detail of rudder linkage, motor and coupling together with servo mounting on the model tug Cruiser.

Rudder and propeller detail on Cruiser.

of the ship together with drawings can be found in the previously mentioned book, *British Steam Tugs* by P N Thomas.

The kit is a full kit - i.e. it is complete with all the necessary materials needed to build a complete model except for adhesives and paint. As with most kits, while a propeller and shaft are included, the modeller is required to provide the drive equipment and radio control gear if the model is to be made operative.

Ballast in the form of lead sheet or similar heavy material is also needed to load the model to its waterline. It should be mentioned also that, while a scale tow hook is included, this model is not designed for actual towing - for example, in a tug-towing competition - as the hook is of white metal parts and is attached to the detachable superstructure. If the completed model is to be used for actual towing then the builder must find some alternative position near the stern of the ship for a second tow hook, and ensure that this hook is of adequate strength and very securely fixed to the hull of the model.

As the description of building this kit proceeds, some of the aspects of full-size tug construction and practice will be detailed so that you will, hopefully, gain experience in the history and development of the tug from early times to the present day.

The sequence of building described herein is that used by me and recommended by the kit maker. It is, therefore, the sequence that is best followed by all those new to kit building, but some more experienced modellers may wish to build in a different order and there is no reason why you should not follow your own way. In practice, many parts of a kit need to be constructed and painted before they can be installed, and frequently there are items in a kit which are, in themselves, small kits for building as separate units - among these will be found winches and windlasses, lifeboats etc. The lifeboats, the winches and windlasses can be built at any time during the construction of the model and, after painting, fitted when the time comes. There will be times too when construction of the main

model is held up waiting for glue to cure or paint to dry. Watching paint dry is a very tedious business and such periods of waiting can best be occupied by building one or other of the needed sub-assemblies.

Cruiser, because of its complexity, is not a kit recommended for the novice builder but was chosen for this description because it embodies almost all the tasks and all the detail to be found on the full-size tug - not only of its period but of the modern tug also. The novice, or builder who has little experience of ship modelling, is advised to pick a model more suitable to his/her talents and to gain experience before moving to the more ambitious and costly projects. The model tug *Neptune* illustrated is an example of what can be built by the newcomer to the hobby from a small kit of fairly simple construction by Robbe. This kit is widely available from model shops at a reasonable cost and takes but a short time to build and have an attractive model on the water. Always take time and care when choosing a kit: not all have the same quality or comprehensive contents; not all include the fittings which may form a separate package at extra cost; not all have fully detailed drawings and instructions but all have their good points. Examine the selected kit with the assistance of the shop assistant and, where possible, get advice from a more competent modeller. It is a decided advantage to join a model boat club before embarking upon a project, and to seek advice from the more experienced members before spending what can be quite significant sums on the most agreeable of hobbies - model boating.

Chapter 2   Harbour tugs

As described in the previous chapter, tugs fall into fairly clear categories. The small harbour and river workboat pattern tugs make attractive small models and can be built to larger scales than the bigger tugs which helps when making details - details and small parts of models built to a small scale are more difficult to make than those in a larger scale. Harbour tugs can still be found in service today with some having been built in recent years. In general such tugs are less complex than the larger vessels and therefore are a more suitable type for the modeller of little experience to attempt to build.

With regard to how the harbour tug has changed over the years, there are illustrations in a number of books of paddle tugs for harbour and river use, some of which survived into the middle of the 1970s. As mentioned before, there is but one kit of a paddle tug on the market today and that is *Glasgow*, produced by Graupner in Germany (see Appendix 1). This is a harbour tug and can, I understand, be fitted with a steam outfit of small size although it is usually driven by an electric motor. Within the capability of the newcomer to model shipbuilding, it is not recommended for the novice without any modelling experience at all. The novice builder will be better suited to the single screw type tug such as *Neptune* or the others illustrated within this chapter.

The steam engine was, of course, the prime mover in the earliest tugs and small steam engines and boilers are readily available today from a number of specialist manufacturers. The small harbour tug built from a kit can be outfitted with a steam plant of small size such as are made for the Minivap range of model ships. By present-day standards such steam outfits are not too expensive and can compare reasonably with the more sophisticated electric drive equipment. It is necessary, however, to buy the steam plant from a reputable maker and to ensure that it carries a full set of test certificates as such certificates are required to be shown

The model of the ship handling tug Wyeforce *by Model Slipway.*

to the officials of model clubs before the models may be steamed on the water under their control. More of this will be detailed in later chapters. It would be better for the newcomer and/or novice to fit a simple electric drive for a first model - electric and steam drives are both described later.

With the development of the diesel engine and suitable gearboxes, tugs very quickly converted to this form of propulsion, particularly as the diesel engine can be started and be in service in a few minutes whereas a steam plant needs some hours if the boiler has been allowed to go cold. The gearbox is, of course, essential as the diesel engine cannot be reversed as can the steam unit, and it is through the gearbox that the high speed of the diesel is reduced to the required revolutions for the propeller, in addition to providing the reversing facility. As far as I can ascertain, there are no tugs in service operating with a direct drive from the engine.

Modern harbour tugs such as *Wyeforce* are twin screw-driven having twin diesel engines and gear-

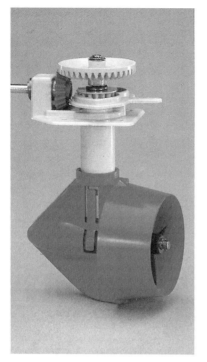
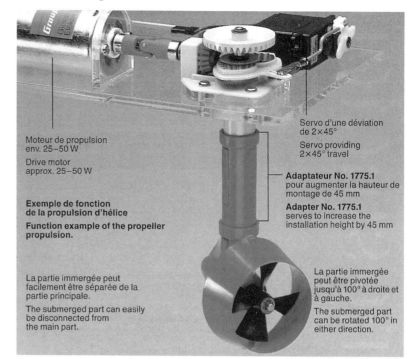

Moteur de propulsion
env. 25–50 W

Drive motor
approx. 25–50 W

**Exemple de fonction
de la propulsion d'hélice**

**Function example of the propeller
propulsion.**

La partie immergée peut
facilement être séparée de la
partie principale.

The submerged part can easily
be disconnected from
the main part.

Servo d'une déviation
de 2×45°

Servo providing
2×45° travel

Adaptateur No. 1775.1
pour augmenter la hauteur de
montage de 45 mm

Adapter No. 1775.1
serves to increase the
installation height by 45 mm

La partie immergée
peut être pivotée
jusqu'à 100° à droite et
à gauche.

The submerged part
can be rotated 100° in
either direction.

Shottel drive unit (scale 1:50) by Marx Luder.   *Schottel drive unit by Graupner.*

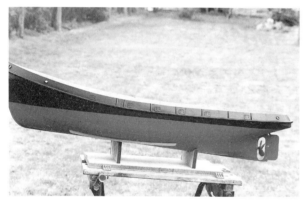

The hull of Cruiser *painted and varnished preparatory to fitting out.*

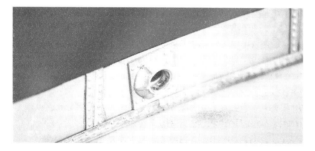

Photo showing the Panama port on the bulwark of Cruiser.

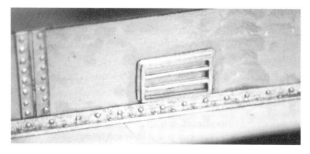

Detail of freeing port in the bulwarks of Cruiser.

boxes. This allows for easy manoeuvring in confined areas and gives the tug the ability to work easily when in close proximity to its main ship. The model illustrated comes from The Model Slipway range of kits (see Appendix 1) and is a popular model among model tug-towing enthusiasts. The kit can be completed fairly quickly by the competent modeller and, when outfitted with good drive motors, can provide a good bollard pull. Bollard pull is the measuring yardstick by which tugs are compared. Each tug, when on trials, is required to haul against a static bollard with equipment that can calculate, in tons, how strongly the ship pulls and this information is then available to all who need it. One model *Wyeforce* known to me was found to be capable of a bollard pull of 4.5 lb measured with a spring balance with the model running full ahead.

Many modern harbour tugs today seem to be fitted with one of two differing drive systems: the azimuth thruster or the Voith Schneider propeller. Both of these types of propulsion permit the ship to move in any direction under bridge control. These drive systems are not peculiar to tugs and can also be found on other types of ship. Neither the azimuth thruster or the Voith Schneider propeller system are available in model form although working Voith units were, for a short while, produced by Graupner. The nearest model unit to the azimuth thruster is the Schottel drive (illustrated here) being almost identical to the azimuth thruster, but only capable of being revolved through 240 degrees as against the azimuth unit which can turn through a complete circle. This unit is made by Marx Luder and

A model of the period steam tug Furie *used on harbour duty on the European continent* (photo courtesy Deans Marine).

equates to a scale of 1:50 - similar units are available from other makers but seem to be to the same scale, which, naturally, restricts their use to models built to this scale. Incidentally, as far as I know, there are no kits currently being made which incorporate any other than the conventional screw propeller drives.

Cruiser - running gear and hull painting

Continuing with the description of building a kit model tug, *Cruiser* came in a very large box containing a hull in grp which carries plate detail, timber sections for deck beams and supports, fine plywood in two thicknesses for decks etc., superstructure, funnel and two lifeboats moulded in grp, and a host of fittings cast in white metal together with material for the boat covers and bridge screening, vacuum-formed lenses for the navigation lamps and various thicknesses and colours of rigging cord. The instruction manual is well printed and bound, and the large, single sheet drawing is of full size for the model. Almost all kit makers who include hulls moulded in grp will recommend that the hulls be washed in hot water and detergent to remove any remaining release agent used in manufacture, and that the hull should be lightly rubbed all over with fine (400 grit) wet-and-dry abrasive paper to provide a key for the subsequent painting. It should also be noted that, once the hull has been so treated, it should not be handled with bare hands as grease

from fingers will seriously impede satisfactory adhesion of paint coats. If necessary, degrease the hull with methylated spirit or cellulose thinners on a soft cloth and allow it to dry before applying the paint.

Before reaching the hull painting stage, however, other tasks need to be done. While the hull is open it is best to install the propeller shaft, line up the drive equipment (electric motor or steam engine) with a suitable coupling, temporarily fit the propeller and make provision for the drive motor or engine mounting. These can be installed after the main deck is fitted but the task is much easier in the open hull. In the case of *Cruiser* the selected motor was a Marx Luder Decaperm, driving the propeller shaft through a single Huco coupling - shaft, coupling and motor being very carefully aligned and the motor screwed down firmly to a timber base that was subsequently sealed into the hull. The cast propeller supplied with the kit was fitted to a length of mild steel rod, threaded at one end to accept it and then suspended on two knife-blade edges to check it for truth in balance. It was found to be out of balance and small quantities of metal were filed from the back of some of the blades until the unit balanced as perfectly as possible on the knife edges. It was then tried on the hull.

Mention has not been made of the cast framework that carries the rudder post, sits over the propeller shaft and fits to the bottom of the keel at the stern

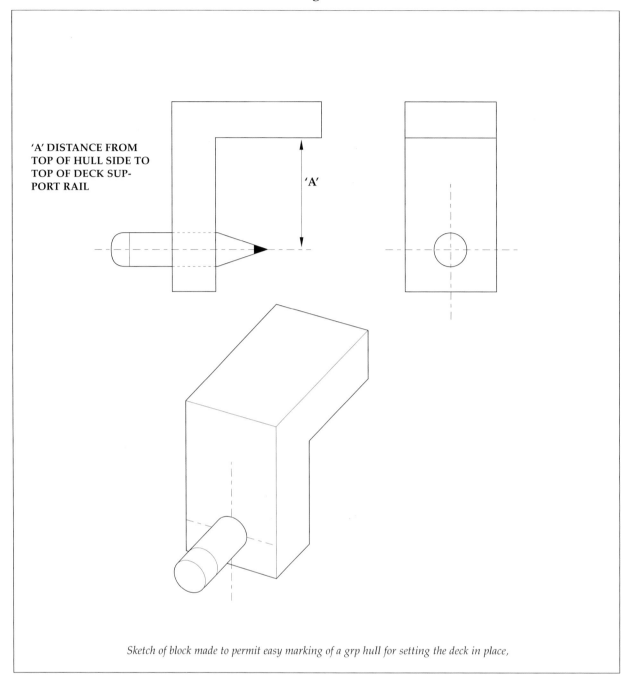

'A' DISTANCE FROM TOP OF HULL SIDE TO TOP OF DECK SUPPORT RAIL

'A'

Sketch of block made to permit easy marking of a grp hull for setting the deck in place,

and to the underside of the stern close to the rudder stock upper bearing location. This is a large, quite heavy casting and care is needed to fit it accurately. Cyanoacrylate (superglue) was used to tack the casting in place but, after checking the fit, it was finally secured with 24-hour epoxy and all gaps were filled with a P38-type car body filler. The rudder is also a white metal casting supplied complete with the stock fitted and it needs to have the slots for the bearings opened up so that it can be secured using mock fastenings at the top and middle but a properly made and bolted bearing and shaft at the bottom. Using a small bolt with a nut to form the bottom-bearing pintle does allow the rudder to be removed for attention when necessary. At the top of the rudder stock inside the hull the brass bearing tube was reinforced with a

small block of wood, drilled to fit over the tube and secured with 24-hour epoxy. As the rudder assembly is quite heavy a closed circuit rod and clevis system was fitted to connect to the rudder servo as this would impose less strain on the servo and allow the fitting of a push on/push off switch to control the smoke units that were to be fitted into the funnel -   more details of this will follow in later chapters.

To complete work on the hull before the main deck was laid, the cast rings for the Panama ports and the doors of the water release openings were fitted using superglue. These were very fine castings and do enhance the hull sides. The next task was the fitting of the bilge keels, the locations for which are clearly marked on the hull.

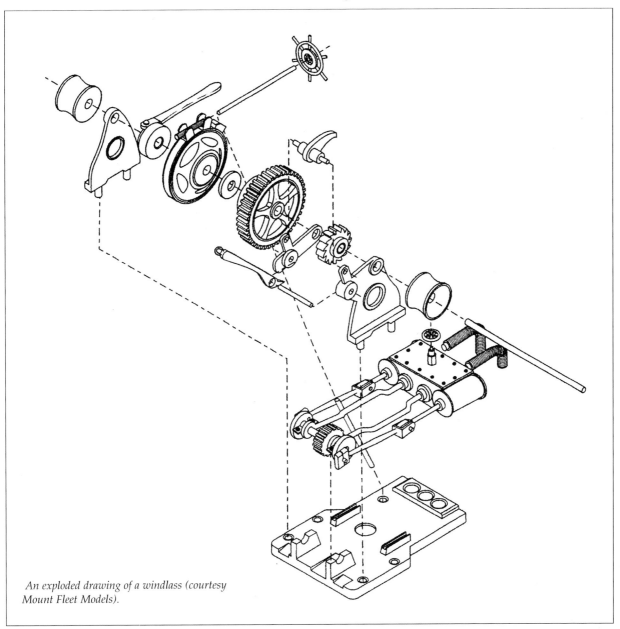

An exploded drawing of a windlass (courtesy Mount Fleet Models).

The instructions for fitting these keels made from marked out 1.5mm plywood are quite explicit and would not cause problems for any builder, but I decided to fit the keels in my own way by cutting slots in the hull, inserting the pre-cut keels through the slots and securing them inside the hull with body filler. Reinforcing timber of 2mm square section was used under each keel to help support the ply keels and to cover and seal any openings left by the process. The timber of the keels was sealed with two coats of sanding sealer and sanded to a smooth finish.

The hull was next prepared for painting as previously described and was given three coats of red oxide primer from a spray can - the preferred type being acrylic car spray primer from Halfords. After application each coating was examined and any blemishes sanded away or holes filled and sanded smooth before applying the succeeding coat. Some seven days were allowed to elapse before the next stage was attempted so that the primer had a good chance of being fairly well cured. The hull was mounted upon a stand on the flat surface of the workbench and checked for vertical alignment. It was then propped up carefully so that the waterline positions at bow and stern, taken from the drawings, were equidistant from the bench. The waterline was marked with a sharply pointed, soft pencil clamped to an engineer's square which was drawn round the hull and firmly held to the bench while the point of the pencil drew the line on the hull. The line was checked on both sides of the hull to ensure that the hull had not moved during the process. The hull was next masked off below the drawn waterline with good quality masking tape and newsprint, care being taken to ensure that the tape at the pencil line was well smoothed down to avoid paint leaching down beneath the tape. The

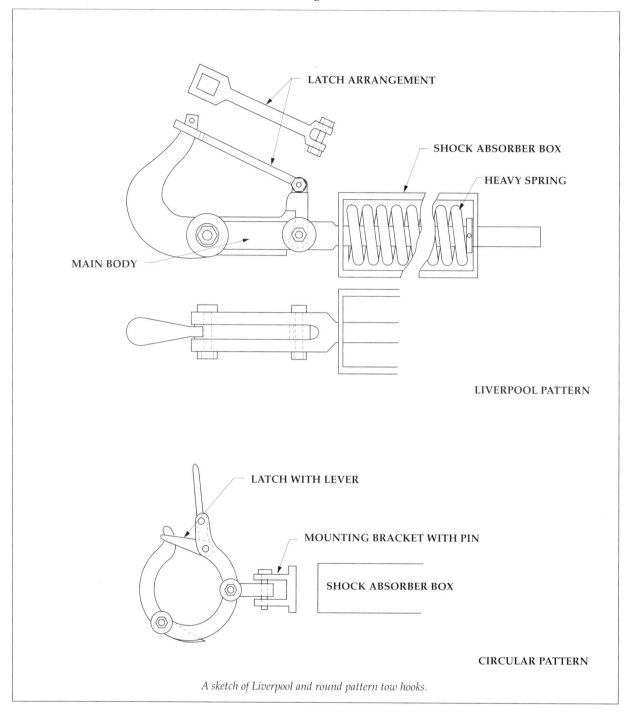

A sketch of Liverpool and round pattern tow hooks.

upper hull was then given three coats of acrylic black primer from a spray can, also from Halfords, and set aside to dry out for a few days. During the drying periods other work was carried out on such items as the lifeboat davits etc. which could be considered small kits in themselves and which could be made, painted and set aside until needed.

Further work on this kit model follows in successive chapters.

Chapter 3   Coastal tugs

Estuary and coastal tugs such as may be used for moving large vessels quite long distances between ports or up the bigger estuaries, for example the Humber, Bristol Channel etc. are different, in many ways, from their smaller harbour sisters. Usually such tugs have a degree of accommodation to permit the crew to live on board for a short period during an extended towing duty. They are, obviously, larger than the harbour tug, fitted with more powerful engines and frequently carry two tow hooks of different sizes to accommodate the range of vessels they may have to handle. Generally, they have high bows and a deep sheer to permit them to work in heavy weather and high seas reasonably safely. *Cruiser* is an example of a coastal tug.

In the early days of the tug, the accommodation was very spartan indeed, the whole idea of the tug being that of a workhorse with little thought to the comfort of the crew. The tug was little more than a vehicle for a large and powerful engine with its accompanying boiler plant. This condition prevailed from the early days right up to shortly after World War Two when many aspects of Merchant Navy life were changed by legislation. The modern coastal tug is much better geared to the comfort of the crew with more thought given to the working conditions of the men. The tug master has a great responsibility towards his tow and its value - he needs to be fully aware of the effect of wind, tide and current on his tow, particularly if it is not under some degree of power. His expertise must include knowledge of the estuaries, rivers and coasts in which he trades and, above all, he must know the capabilities of his tug to the last possible degree. Today, with so few tugs in service, the range of duties for the coastal tug have been seriously depleted and there is a tendency for the modern

Odin - *a model harbour tug from a Robbe kit* (photo courtesy Robbe Schluter UK).

tug to be designed, not only for harbour duty but for coastal service too.

In the days of the steam screw and paddle tugs the distinction between the various types of tugs was quite marked, but today there is often very little to choose between them other than size. There are kits available to build models of some of these types of tug as the illustrations show, some covering single screw tugs and some twin screw units - one is of the paddle tug Glasgow produced by Graupner. Within the ranges of the continental European makers will be found a few tugs, the biggest range being from Billings (see Appendix 1) who have a number of tugs of varying sizes and duties in their catalogue. In fact, the very first model ship I constructed was from a kit of a tug from the Billings range, and one which is still available, called *Zwarte Zee*. This kit included all the necessary timber to build the hull plank-on-frame and it taught me a great deal relative to building hulls from lines drawings - the exercise was more like building from scratch than from a boxed kit although the inclusion of an instruction manual did measurably assist construction.

When buying a kit do ask advice from the shop, particularly if you are new to the hobby. A good many kits are quite complex and, unless the buyer has some modelling experience, it is not unknown for a kit to be started and then discarded because he/she had insufficient experience to overcome some of the complexities. The coastal tug was a common sight in almost all the ports of reasonable size in the years after World War Two - they were almost always the pride and joy of their masters and crew and were kept in fine condition. In the same manner as the larger merchant ships, most tugs sported funnel colours and insignia relative to their owners and they could be recognised from a distance by such colours. It was helpful to the captains and crews of ships to be able to see their expected tugs from a distance so that they could be ready to accept the towing hawser, and also to know that a rival tug was not trying to pick up a tow.

Cruiser - main decks and bulwarks

Continuing the construction notes for *Cruiser*, once the hull paint had had a reasonable time for drying, a stand was constructed to carry the hull while further work was carried out. A good stand is essential and is easily made from plywood or chipboard of about 10mm to 15mm thickness. The curved ends that take the weight of the hull should be covered with thick felt or similar cloth so that the paintwork is not damaged. A good stand will hold the model firmly and, while it will

Al Khubar. *The very latest model tug kit from Model Slipway features twin screws in nozzles and rubber tyres* (photo courtesy Model Slipway).

Active - *a small harbour tug from a kit by Mount Fleet Models* (photo courtesy Mount Fleet Models).

be needed at the waterside to hold the boat until it is placed in the water, it will also be very useful for display purposes if and when the model is put into a competition or exhibition. The photographs show the working model stand made for *Cruiser*.

The kit instructions and materials included for *Cruiser* made no mention of the ship having a camber to the deck and thus the model illustrated was built without deck camber. It is most unlikely that the decks of the tug were flat but in the absence of data for this I decided to build the ship precisely to the kit instructions, the only deviations from the kit contents were the fitting of illumination to the navigation lights and the inclusion of twin smoke generators in the base of the funnel. The 10mm x 10mm square stripwood provided was fitted round the insides of the hull at the level of the main deck with allowance being made for the thickness of the deck material. A neat means of marking off the deck was shown in the instructions and the sketch here illustrates how a soft pencil can be fitted into a small, simple frame to permit the deck location to be accurately marked. The timber was secured to the hull with catalysed, polyester resin gelcoat which is

Detail of bulwark supports on the model Cruiser.

Coamings built up for Cruiser *superstructure.*

thixotropic, of the same formula as the grp hull and which creates a firm bond in about twenty minutes in a warm atmosphere. At bow and stern strips of 5.0mm thick styrene were used as they conform to the curves more easily than the timber would. These strips were applied in two layers, the first being secured by the gelcoat and the sec- ond glued over the first using liquid polystyrene cement. While ten to twenty minutes is long enough to create a good bond with these adhe- sives, full cure is not effected for less than 12 hours, thus it is wise to do this part of the work late on one day and set the model overnight to cure before proceeding further. Beams running athwartships (across the hull) are cut from the 10mm x 10 mm stripwood to fit at the locations given in the instructions. These were secured with two-part epoxy resin and small triangles of scrap ply were used to reinforce each joint as is shown in the photographs. Once more, time must elapse before the hull can be handled and while the adhesive cures. This time can be adequately filled by building, for example, the windlass for the foredeck. The windlass is built from a set of castings and short pieces of brass rod and wire; the task itself is pleasurable as the cast parts require very little attention other than polishing with a fine wire brush. A brush such as is used for cleaning suede shoes is ideal for cleaning and polishing white metal parts prior to gluing or painting.

The drawing shown here clearly shows the windlass assembly and the photographs illustrate the finished item. The kit instructions suggest that the parts are given a coat of white primer before being painted in the appropriate colours and this is excellent advice. This windlass was primed with acrylic paint from Halfords. Once completed the windlass was placed carefully away until it could be fitted to the model. The barred chain which comes as separate cast links needs to be assembled and painted too, preparatory to fitting on the model.

The decks of the tug were marked out on 1.5mm thick marine ply in two sections, fore and aft. Each

was first cut out from the timber sheet and then tried on the model. Here some work is needed to get the plywood parts to fit closely to the hull sides, but using a spokeshave and a sanding block the decks did eventually fit neatly. At amidships they were allowed to overlap so that they could be marked for cutting and it is wise to ensure that the joint between the two deck sections falls at the centre of a deck beam. I did not allow for this and consequently needed to fit an additional beam to carry the decks where they joined athwartships. Before the decks were glued down to the beams the undersides were sealed with sanding sealer and given two coats of paint against possible deterioration due to dampness. Such sealing is particularly essential where the model is to be outfitted with a steam plant. It is not necessary to seal the upper surfaces of the plywood which will subsequently be covered. In addition the centres of both deck sections were cut away to form the access to the hull when the superstructure is removed. To ensure that sufficient deck was cut away the preformed superstructure was placed on the deck and carefully set to the correct location by measuring from the drawings. A line was drawn round the deckhouse unit on the deck and the two deck sections were then trimmed to within 1.0mm of the drawn lines.

Following the kit instructions the deck beams were cut away in way of the deck opening and coamings were made and fitted to hold the super-

The vintage American harbour tug Seguin *built from a Midwest kit and fitted with a single cylinder steam outfit.*

structure in place and to render the opening in the deck fairly watertight when the deckhouse is fitted. Such coamings or upstands round deck openings prevent water washing under the deckhouses or hatches and into the interior of the model. The decks of the model were glued down with water resistant PVA adhesive and weights were used to hold the decks down until the glue cured. The coamings were similarly glued with PVA and allowed to dry. Within the kit contents was a large sheet of fine quality white card to be used to 'plate' the decks. Cruiser had decks of steel plate which were painted with red oxide but otherwise left untreated, and such plating was simulated using the white card cut into suitably sized pieces. In two places, immediately forward and immediately aft of the superstructure, the deck was covered in asphalt and this was simulated with two pieces of 0.8mm thick plywood cut and shaped to fit between the bulwarks. Card and ply were both glued with PVA and weighted to hold them firm until the adhesive had cured. Once all this work on the decks was complete they were given two coats of sanding sealer and lightly sanded, followed by three coats of red oxide primer from a spray can. After each application of paint the decks and coamings were examined and any blemishes found were made good before the next coating. Good surface finish with paint needs care and attention to the surface before any paint is applied, and requires continuing attention during the various applications of the paint.

The next task was to fit all the Panama port rings and the relief doors to the inside of the bulwarks and to prepare, mark off and fit all the riveted butt plates. All these fittings are formed in white metal and a little cleaning was necessary before they were attached with superglue to the bulwarks. At regular intervals round the bulwarks stays need to be fitted, each stay comprising two cast, white metal parts, the lower part having a peg to fit into a pre-drilled hole in the deck. This task needed careful measurement - some 44 stays are located round the perimeter of the deck and at differing spacings - and constant reference to the main drawing was essential. As the back of each stay is inaccessible once the stay is fitted they were all painted with red oxide before being glued in place with superglue. No attempt was made to trim the stays to correct height until all had been fitted and were firmly secured, then the tops were cut away and filed flush to the bulwark top. The top rails were next cut from 0.8mm plywood very carefully to conform to the curves of the bulwarks and glued down with superglue, the tops of the stays helping to hold the rails level. Weights were used to hold the rails in place until the glue set. These bulwark rails are flush to

the outside of the bulwarks and were sanded until they lay correctly.

Once the rails were secure they were treated with sanding sealer and sanded smooth, and subsequently painted black by hand using acrylic paints (Humbrol). Acrylic paints were used in preference to oil-based colours as the brushes can be washed out in water and they rarely show brush marks. All the paints needed for *Cruiser* were of acrylic composition and some colours were mixed up to suit. Having completed the bulwarks both inside and out, the whole hull and decks were given two coats of matt varnish from a spray and the model was set aside to thoroughly dry.

The making and fitting of deck items can be done at almost any stage of building the model and, while waiting for the varnish treatment on the hull to dry, various deck fittings were made and prepared for fitting. One particular fitting found on all but the very largest of salvage tugs is the tow hook and its associated frame. In general there are two types of hook used in the UK and Europe, both of which are illustrated here. Cruiser was fitted with the Liverpool pattern hook which was built up from a series of cast white metal parts. As with all the white metal fittings, there was little flash to remove and mainly the parts needed to be polished with the small suede brush before being glued together with superglue. However, if you wish to use your model in tug-towing regattas and competitions then the tow hook or towing arrangements need to be very strongly constructed and certainly not made from white metal castings. I would suggest that a towing hook of brass be made and secured to the hull in some way or that a towing bollard be built and anchored to the hull. This may not comply strictly with the scale aspect of the model but such cannot be avoided if tug towing is to be the object of building the model.

Other items of deck furniture such as skylights, bollards and fairleads, which come with the kit, can be treated to suitable painting before being located and fitted. Small gooseneck vents and dip pipes for the deep tanks can also be made and fitted, these being easily fashioned from scraps of brass rod if they do not form part of the kit contents.

Most tugs carry one lifeboat and often two, mounted under davits of one kind or another - various types of davits are illustrated through successive chapters. The more modern coastal or harbour tugs are fitted with rigid inflatable boats for lifesaving and usually they carry a small dinghy for ferrying the crew ashore when the ship is at the buoys or at anchor. Lifeboats and dinghies are delightful small models in themselves and can be purchased in ready-made form from some specialists, or purchased in kit form from most model ship shops (see Appendix 2). As an exercise they can fill an evening or two building from scratch. Regretfully the only two books of which I am cognisant relating to the building and detailing of small boats are both out of print. The Ship Model Maker's Manual by John Bowen (Arco Publishing Inc., New York) is a treasury of shipboard detail and Model Open Boats by Ewart C Freeston (Conway Maritime Press) covers the building of small boats in great detail. Hopefully your local

library services may be able find copies for your information - my own copies are regular sources of reference. There are, of course, many books on ships and ship modelling available in the bookshops (including many published by Nexus Special Interests) today which, without doubt, will contain data of value to the model shipbuilder. You should consult as many sources of reference as possible when building a model ship in the interests of accuracy, if for no other reason. Researching into a particular ship for the purposes of building a model can be a fascinating time and you can learn a great deal from such researches.

Chapter 4   Estuary tugs and tug tenders

Next up the scale from the coastal tug came the estuary tug and tug tender. They were not necessarily larger than the coastal but were somewhat more specialised. In the days of the large liners that regularly made ocean-wide voyages almost to an exact timetable, there were ports or calls where it was impossible for the liner to dock due to its size and the port facilities or time taken to dock the ship was too costly. Passengers and their often large quantities of luggage were ferried out to the liner in tugs specially built to accommodate such passengers in addition to their tug-towing duties. To the best of my knowledge there are only two kits available depicting tug tenders - *Alte Liebe* and *Westbourne* - both by Caldercraft. Both are tugs which were steam-driven and were quite small, neither being large enough to ferry passengers out to large liners anchored in the roads off shore. The larger tenders such as *Romsey* and *Flying Kestrel* (illustrated in British Steam Tugs by P N Thomas) were fitted with large lounges and saloons for the comfort of transit passengers. To build such passenger-carrying tugs you will need to start from scratch, seek and find

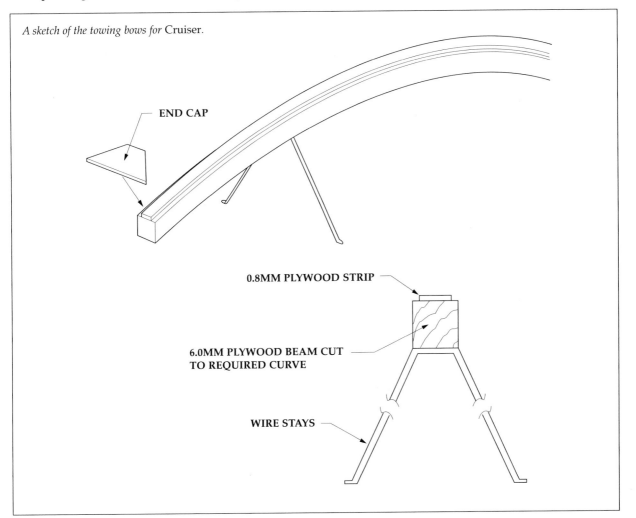

A sketch of the towing bows for Cruiser.

END CAP

0.8MM PLYWOOD STRIP

6.0MM PLYWOOD BEAM CUT TO REQUIRED CURVE

WIRE STAYS

suitable drawings and research into the details and painting of the ships.

In the early days of the steam tug owners frequently carried passengers between ports on the same river or estuary as a means of supplementing the ship's earnings. These early tugs were not equipped for carrying passengers but they just had to make the best of it. In addition, passenger steamers were not equipped for towing but they often did so in order to gain extra income. The whole scene was one of fierce competition.

Almost every town close to the sea ran paddle tug trips around the bay and very often the tugs were dangerously overloaded. The tug tender really came into its own when passenger liners became too large to go alongside the quays in some ports until serious alterations and dredging was carried out. It was then, in the late 1870s, that two steam tugs were built specifically to service large liners and to carry passengers and their belongings out to the ships which lay to anchor off the port or river. The first of these special tugs was built for Steel and McCaskill, the forerunners of Steel and Bennie who owned the tug *Cruiser* (the model of which is being described herein).

On some rivers such as the Clyde the ferrying of passengers to the large liners was generally left in the hands of the pleasure steamers which abounded on the Clyde and which numbered some very fine ships indeed. Elsewhere, such as Queenstown in southern Ireland, the tug tender

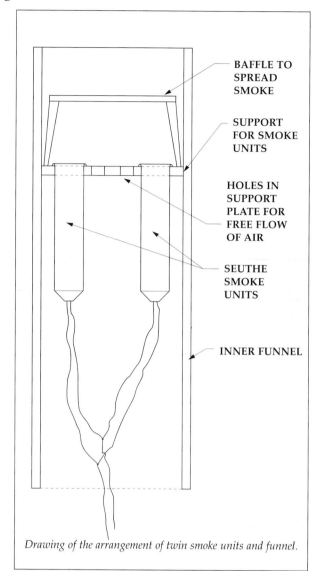

BAFFLE TO SPREAD SMOKE

SUPPORT FOR SMOKE UNITS

HOLES IN SUPPORT PLATE FOR FREE FLOW OF AIR

SEUTHE SMOKE UNITS

INNER FUNNEL

Drawing of the arrangement of twin smoke units and funnel.

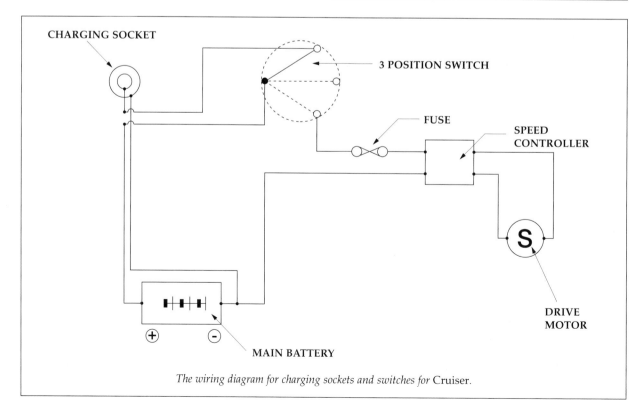

CHARGING SOCKET

3 POSITION SWITCH

FUSE

SPEED CONTROLLER

S

DRIVE MOTOR

MAIN BATTERY

The wiring diagram for charging sockets and switches for Cruiser.

The harbour tug/tender Alte Leibe *(photo courtesy Jotika).*

Westbourne - *a small tug/tender from the Caldercraft range* (photo courtesy Jotika).

Passengers could have been carried on the Seguin *but it is not known if this was the case.*

rails and other fine details found mainly on passenger liners of the day.

Much of the pleasure in building model ships comes from making a model which is unique and specifically one's own. However, most modellers have neither the time nor the facilities to build a model from the builder's drawings, and neither do they wish to spend time and effort in making extensive researches into the particular ship. The kit model provides the quickest way to get a model on the water and, in general, the research work needed has already been carried out by the kit maker before the kit is marketed. It is possible, with a little care, thought and attention to make the kit model unique to the builder. Careful examination of full-size ships will often show where a slight modification will make a model different from that shown on the box lid. Often the model in the kit had sister ships which were similar but with slight differences and such differences can be incorporated into the model as it is built to give a different ship. Sometimes it is not possible to find the ship you require in full kit form, in which case it might be available from a specialist supplier as a detailed grp hull complete with a set of drawings. As mentioned previously, a number of suppliers provide what are known as semi-kits which comprise a grp hull, drawings and packaged sets of fittings with which to detail the model. No material is provided for decks, superstructures, masts, etc. all of which, including the propeller(s) and shaft(s), must be bought separately. This system does allow you to buy only what you need initially and to purchase fittings as they are needed thus spreading the cost over much of the building time. This system, too, does allow you to build a model which is special to you alone.

The driving of the ship model is a matter of personal choice often controlled by the depth of the pocket. It has been my rule throughout life to buy the very best tools and equipment I possibly could on the basis that the best lasts longest and is, in the long run, the cheapest. In this manner, most of the working models built by me have been outfitted with either electric motors from the Marx Luder range or steam plants from either Cheddar Models or Maxwell Hemmens, now known as John Burrell Engineers. In both cases the choice has been dictated by quality in preference to price, rarely has a Decaperm, Hectaperm or Monoperm motor failed in service or to do the job for which it was intended. In the same way, the steam plants of Cheddar Models and John Burrell have also given no cause for worry or doubt of their ability to perform their required duties. There are, however, a range of much less expensive motors and steam outfits on the market today and these

was a part of the daily scene. Some shipowners at ports such as Liverpool, Southampton etc., had tug/tenders specially built to serve their own fleets. Cunard, for example, had a number of such vessels and a great deal of detail relative to such ships can be found within British Steam Tugs by P N Thomas. It is a shame that no kit manufacturer has yet included a tug/tender of the passenger-carrying type such as *Skirmisher*, owned by Cunard and which, in some respects, resembled an ocean liner as it was built with wood-topped

A typical steam outfit from the Cheddar models range.

A steam outfit from the Stour Valley Steam range.

ranges are expanding as demand increases. Many of these cheaper alternatives have their place in the model ship world and it would be wrong for anyone to denigrate these products. It is wise, however, to consider fitting a reduction gearbox between the motor and the propeller shaft - high speeds only create cavitation and cause the propeller to slip without providing the required degree of thrust. With the smaller, cheaper high-speed motors the net result is high current consumption if a gear reduction system is not installed. With a steam plant a reduction gear system is not usually necessary unless the steam engine is of particularly high speed. Further details of gear drives, motors and steam engines are to be found in later chapters.

Cruiser - deck and interior fittings

Returning to *Cruiser*, having completed the hull painting and fitted the deck coverings, many of the deck fittings such as the anchor windlass, bollards and fairleads etc. can be fitted. With the model pictured, holes were drilled in the anchor recess in the hull and in the deck at the prescribed location, and a 6.0mm bore brass tube was cut and sealed in place to form the hawse pipe. The anchor, having been assembled and painted white was attached to the length of stud link chain, also painted white, and drawn up the pipe into the hawse box. The chain cable was fitted carefully over the chain drum of the windlass and down through a hole in the deck under the windlass. It was then secured with a few drops of superglue and the result can be seen in some of the pictures. Tugs did not often use an anchor but tended to lie to buoys in the river, harbour or estuary. Lying alongside a quay generally was more costly than lying to buoys and it was an easy matter to lower the dinghy and row to the shore - not so easy to return to the ship if one had imbibed a dram too much although very few crew members were known to drown through falling into the water under the influence!

An illustration of an anchor windlass clearly visible on this model of Sandra, *a Thames-type tug model built by Edward Heller from the USA from a Marvon Models kit.*

The stern of Cruiser *showing the capstan, gobeye and grating over the rudder quadrant etc.*

The engine-room casing on Cruiser *showing towing bows, stove chimney and the tall cowl ventilator.*

Tug crews were, and are, hard working and hard men, skilled in all aspects of their work and usually proud of their vessels. This pride showed in the way their ships were turned out but even more so in the state of the engines which, on all I have seen, gleamed and sparkled. The gentle thudding of the pistons and almost silent tapping of the valves of the modern oil engines can be heard as a tug passes, the sound being indicative of the care and attention which is lavished upon the machinery. In the same way, care and attention to the machinery of the model tug will repay the owner many times over.

Cruiser has but one anchor although there is an anchor davit, davit locations and rope rings to allow the davit to be positioned on either side of the bows thus allowing the anchor to be lifted up and lowered on the port side through a port in the bulwark. In normal service the anchor would be drawn hard up into the anchor pocket and the cable and windlass locked. It would be possible on the full-size ship to use the rope drums to warp the ship to the quay or other position as the warping drums could be used independently of the chain drum. At the stern, the deck was completed by fitting the capstan, gob-eye or stirrup and rope cradle. The capstan, powered by steam with the engine beneath the covers on the deck, was used to haul in hawsers and ropes and to move the tug in confined spaces. Running round both sides of the stern from the steering engine at the stern of the superstructure to the rudder quadrant are the steering rods and chains which transmit the movement of the steering engine to the massive rudder. On the model this system of chains and rods is not functional but is visible, although the rudder quadrant itself is hidden beneath the grating which is made up from plywood (pre-printed) and white metal gratings. All the necessary guides, pulleys and parts needed to complete the steering system are provided in the kit.

The final fitting for the stern of the tug is the towing bow which runs from side to side and over which the tow rope would be guided so that it could not foul any deck fittings. The method described in the instruction manual seemed to be somewhat complex and it was made from a piece of 6.0mm thick ply cut to the required curve and length and fitted on top with a strip of 0.8mm ply to simulate the timber top. In full-size practice, this bow would have been made from a length of steel channel or 'H' section with the top being closed in and timber sections bolted in place, then finally finished with a hardwood top. The ply bow was fitted with the necessary stays formed from brass rod and the ends of the bow were finished with small pieces of ply as shown in the sketches. The bow was fixed into two shaped pillars, one on each side of the hull, and these pillars set the bow just above the level of the bulwark top rail. The assembly was finally painted black. Of the remaining fittings at the stern, these were built up from the parts provided and comprised a galley stove pipe chimney and a fairly tall ventilator; neither were fitted at this stage as it was felt that the superstructure might foul and cause them to be damaged as it was being removed at frequent intervals during construction.

Before proceeding to construct the superstructure, which is quite complex, the interior of the model was completed. A plate of 3.0mm ply was cut to fit across the hull, just aft of the motor position, to carry the steering servo and this was fixed with brass screws to two 10mm x 10mm square beams fastened to the hull with catalysed polyester resin. The steering servo was fitted through the hole cut in the plate and attached to the tiller of the rudder with a closed circuit system of rods and clevises as can be seen in the pictures and as previously described. On this plate too, was fixed a small switch of the push on/ push off pattern, set so that with the rudder trim on the transmitter at full deflection the arm on the steering servo would push over the switch but when the trim on the transmitter is in the usual central position the switch would not be operated. This switch was wired into the circuit controlling the smoke units

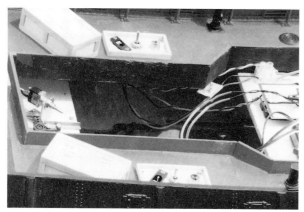

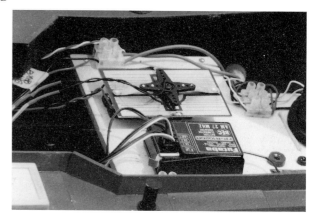

The after section of access to the interior of Cruiser *illustrating the rudder servo and switch for the smoke units, also the switchgear and charging sockets on the deck for the main and radio batteries.*

Detail of the radio receiver, speed control board and connections for Cruiser. *Cables were subsequently tied into a 'loom' with spiral binding.*

to give independent control with only a two-channel radio system. More details and a wiring diagram are provided later for the smoke system.

Forward of the steering platform unit and just forward of the motor position, a second platform was made from 3.0mm ply and screwed down to two 10mm x 10 mm beams fixed to the sides of the hull. This platform was designed to take the radio receiver, the electronic speed controller for the motor and the connection blocks for the electric wiring. At the forward end and amidships a large hole was cut in the plate to accept the funnel of the smoke system, this funnel being sited to come exactly under and just inside the funnel of the model. It was made from the tube of a silicon bath sealant which was cleaned out and cut to the required length. A disc of 3.0mm plywood drilled to accept two small Seuthe smoke units (6 volts) was glued inside the tube and extra holes were drilled to allow air to pass through the ply disc. The cables from the smoke units were joined into two connectors on the ply plate and further connectors and cables connected between the small lead acid battery, the switch near the steering servo and the smoke units - all as shown in the accompanying diagram.

Smoke oil was placed in the units and the system tried out. It gave a satisfactory plume of smoke as

can be seen in some of the photographs showing the model on the water.

As the superstructure is complex and could be damaged by frequent removal at the pond side I decided to fit switches, sockets and indicator lights in two places on the main deck on either side of the model: one to switch in the radio and for the adjacent socket to be used to charge the radio battery pack of Ni-cad batteries and the second to switch in the main drive battery and for the adjacent socket to be used to charge the battery. It is thus possible to set the model in motion and to charge the batteries without removing the superstructure. Both of the switches used are centre off two-way switches, one direction switching in the batteries and the other allowing the batteries to be charged. Each unit is also fitted with a small red lamp to indicate when the circuit is alive to sailing. The wiring diagram for these circuits is given here. It will be noted from the pictures that there is some ballast made from lead sheet fixed in the hull. This ballast was not fitted until the model was completed and it will be detailed in a later chapter.

Once all the fittings were attached to the main deck it was given a couple of coats of matt varnish and set aside to dry thoroughly, most of the work on the superstructure being carried out away from the hull.

Chapter 5   Ocean-going and salvage tugs

Ocean-going tugs were an obvious step up from the coastal and river tugs of the early days; there were some paddle-driven ocean-going tugs but they were not a success any more than the paddle-driven liners of the day. The development of the screw propeller and the reciprocating steam engine led to the building of larger tugs expressly for going 'deep sea'. The Liverpool tugs *Knight of the Cross* and *Knight of St. John*, built in the late 1800s were typical ocean-going tugs of their day. They had twin funnels set closely together, were twin screw-driven and were reputed to be fine sea ships. Some shipbuilders specialised in building tugs. Wm. Simons of Renfrew was one of the most prolific of tug builders, while Redhead's of South Shields and Cochrane's of Selby were regular builders of tugs of all sizes. Here again the steam tug enthusiast is directed to British Steam Tugs by

P N Thomas which is now unfortunately out of print although it is just possible that some bookshops may yet hold stocks.

The model ocean-going and/or salvage tug master is well catered for by the model kit makers. Caldercraft, Model Slipway and Billings all have salvage tugs in their ranges. The producers of hulls in grp also carry ocean-going tug hulls in their ranges and there are many stockists of the various fittings that are needed to complete the model. Most of these very large tugs did not carry towing hooks in the later years as they used the automatic towing winch set usually just under the after end of the superstructure and operated from the bridge. These winches were capable of holding considerable lengths of towing hawser, were suitable for acting as shock absorbers when

Smit Rotterdam - *a model salvage tug from the Billings range* (photo courtesy Amerang Ltd).

taking up the strain of towing from a stop and were used to let out the length of the tow rope when towing in deep ocean waters. An ocean-going tug towing a dead ship over a long sea voyage usually used a tow rope of up to half a mile or more in length. The precise reason for such long distance tow rope is believed to be that it reduces tension per metre, gives more elasticity and therefore is less likely to snap.

The large ocean-going tug or salvage tug frequently covered both duties and carried a great deal of equipment specifically for salvage duty. In the first instance the accommodation was fully enclosed, most passageways between accommodation and working areas were enclosed as protection from inclement weather conditions. There were, usually, some spare cabins for the use of persons who may be rescued and needed to be taken ashore fairly quickly. In recent years all the accommodation would be heated and air conditioned so that the vessel could work in any sea area from the Tropics to the Poles. The need for a salvage tug to get to a ship in distress in a short time frequently caused some design problems as high speed does not also give a good bollard pull, and a good bollard pull is needed for towing purposes. A compromise is almost always the only answer and twin screws allied to reasonable speed is the usual result. Ocean-going, deep-sea,

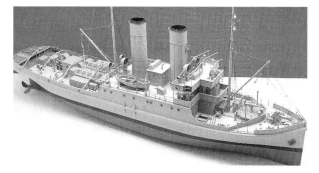

Resolve - *a model of an ocean-going tug for the Admiralty* (photo courtesy Jotika Ltd.)

Yorkshireman - *a salvage tug from the Model Slipway range* (photo courtesy Model Slipway).

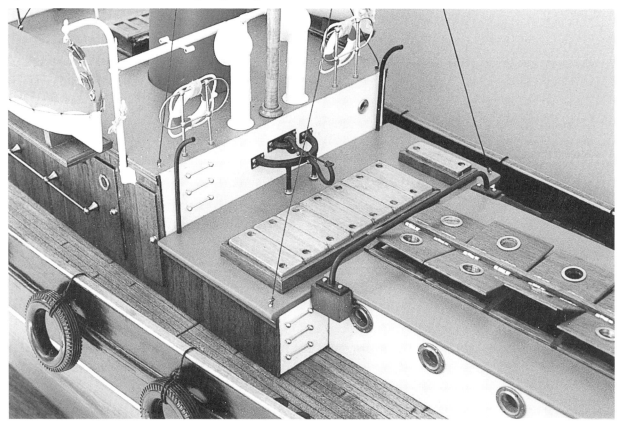

A well-finished model of the Thames tug Sandra *by Edward Heller, clearly illustrating the towing hook, engine-room skylight and coal bunker.*

Ocean-going and salvage tugs

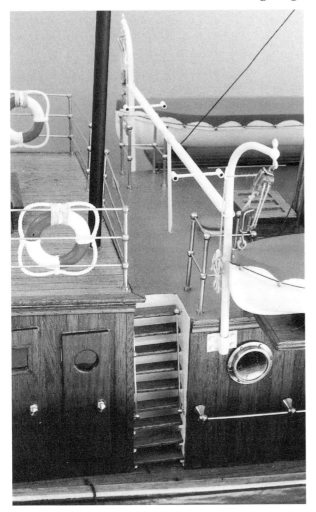

Further superstructure detail on Sandra.

salvage tugs rarely use the azimuth thruster or Voith Schneider propeller but are often fitted with both bow and stern thrusters to give greater manoeuvrability.

Of necessity, these tugs are large and often more than 200 feet in length, they carry such portable items as air compressors and diesel-driven high power pumps which can be lifted on board a damaged ship to assist the ship's own pumps to keep the ship afloat. To handle such large items the tug is generally fitted with a substantial hydraulic crane with a long reach. Among the outfit will be collision mats, welding equipment of both gas and electric pattern, lifejackets, liferafts in containers and all manner of survival equipment to assist in rescuing any personnel involved in the damaged ship.

Salvage is, of course, a lucrative occupation for the tug owners and high fees are paid for the successful salvage of a large vessel that can be repaired and brought back into service. Similar fees are payable for the salvage of cargo and personnel if the cargo reaches a port capable of handling it and it is in good condition - the value of a life is almost incalculable. The modeller building a salvage tug should seek as much information as possible on the vessel in question and enhance the model by the inclusion of such details as salvage machinery which may be stowed on the decks under tarpaulins or in large crates. It is my

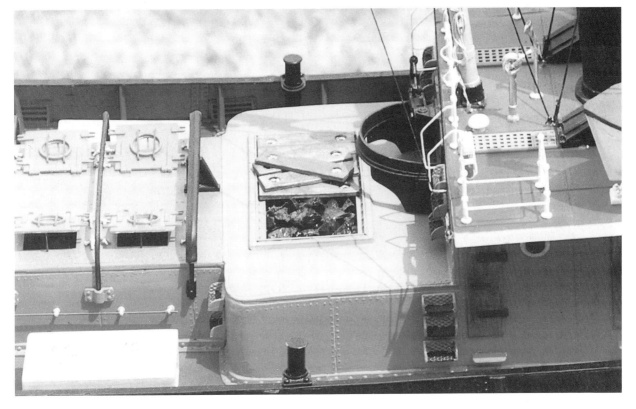

Detail of coal bunker and towing hook frames on Cruiser.

experience that polite requests in writing, accompanied by a self-addressed and stamped envelope for a reply, sent to the owners of a given ship and asking for information to assist in building a model will very often prove fruitful. Many times my letters have resulted in the offer of a visit to the ship and permission to photograph anywhere needful. Such visits are invaluable and give the modeller a real idea of how the full-size ship looks and how it is manned and run.

There are a number of kit manufacturers today who include ocean-going and salvage tugs in their ranges. Many are, of necessity, quite complex and not recommended for the novice or inexperienced ship modeller. In addition, they are usually in the top-of-the-range category where the prices will be quite high. A recent build by a friend of mine occupied some ten months of spare time but resulted in a particularly fine model. Model Slipway, for example, have *Yorkshireman* in their range and Billings list *Smit Rotterdam* both illustrated here and both fine kits for the more experienced builder. Almost all the listed kit manufacturers have a salvage tug or similar in their range and the prospective builder needs to examine and consider the kits offered before reaching a decision. It is, of course, almost impossible for a kit maker to produce a totally fault-free and accurate kit of any given model as the constraints of costs and production methods frequently prevent some parts being made within the selling price budget but, if the vessel is researched carefully, the modeller will most often find that the shortcomings of the kit are easily overcome. The kit is by far the easiest way into building a model ship and additional work after research will compensate for any failings and lead to a fine model in the end.

Cruiser - superstructure (stern part)

Continuing with the building of *Cruiser*, once the main deck with its various fittings was finished it was time to proceed with the superstructure. The kit contains the basic superstructure moulded in grp with much detail moulded in, and it is only necessary to wash the moulding thoroughly with hot water and detergent before proceeding. Initially all the engine-room skylight openings were cut out of the grp by first drilling holes at each corner of the marked light and carefully cutting the opening out with a fine saw. The edges were finished with a file and care was taken to avoid marking the finely moulded detail of rivets etc. In the same manner the marked portholes were drilled out and filed to the correct size. To ensure that each portlight was true, a cast fitting was used to check each one as the work proceeded. The opening for the coal bunker was also cut

away and a false bottom made from spare plywood was installed to which coal could be glued after the base was painted black. This coal bunker arrangement shows clearly in the pictures. It is not necessary to remove the coal bunker top as it can be depicted closed using the timber tops provided. Holes were also cut at the positions of the ventilators on the boat deck and a large hole was cut at the funnel position so that the false funnel with the smoke units would fit neatly beneath. Once again it is not necessary to cut an opening for the funnel unless smoke units are used or, of course, a steam plant is being installed.

Once all the holes have been cut and trued up the whole moulding can be prepared and painted. At this point my method differed from that of the instruction manual. The manual suggested a paint colour mixed from two different standard Humbrol colours but the area of the superstructure is quite large and I felt that tinlets would not go very far and that a fairly large quantity of paint was needed. Fortunately, close by my home, there is a paint company specialising in mixing paint for the local car repair industry and other similar painting contractors, and from this source a large spray can of the required colour with a matt finish was obtained and used for the whole of the work on the superstructure.

Always bear in mind that models are viewed mainly from above and that special care should be given to deck detail, planking and finish of small parts, rails etc. Rails which are not running in straight lines, planking which varies in width etc., all stick out like sore thumbs and spoil the appearance of an otherwise well-finished model. The superstructure was painted at this stage as virtually all the detail to be applied was of white metal castings which needed to be painted once they had been cleaned and before they were fitted. The engine-room skylights for example, were painted white initially and then brown, and were fitted with glazing and protection bars before they were fitted on the model. I decided to show them in the open position - it was very rare to find a steam ship with the engine-room skylights shut, even in wet weather - and the locking bolts and wing nuts were fixed to the deckhead in the open position too. Again this is shown in the photographs.

At the boat deck, wings were fitted made from thin plywood and card and attached to the sides using the cast brackets provided. This task required some care to get the wings level with the main deck and to continue the slight camber of the main section but it looked well when completed. The curtain plates that surround the deck were made from lengths of 0.8mm thick plywood cut to the depths required and fixed in place with super-glue. Curtain plates - so called because they form a curtain pelmet round the edges of decks - are found on almost all ships and they need to be fitted with due attention to the drawings and painted to suit the ship's colour scheme. In the case of Cruiser all the curtain plates are white.

Round the base of the superstructure it was necessary to fit a series of angle plates, cast in white metal and carrying rivet detail. These were each about 75mm long and were glued in place using superglue. They formed a very solid base to the superstructure which sat squarely and neatly over the coamings. It was, of course, necessary to file and sand the bottom edges of the superstructure moulding to obtain an accurate fit between it and the deck before the angle pieces were fitted. Once the flange pieces were fitted and time had been allowed for the adhesive to cure, the whole super-structure unit was given two coats of acrylic grey primer from a spray can followed by three coats of the specially prepared brown. Each coating was carefully examined and any blemishes rectified before the next coat was applied and adequate drying time, of at least two hours, was allowed between coats.

The deck of the coal bunker area was brush painted with grey acrylic once the brown paint had dried, and the curtain plating round the boat deck was painted white. Progressively moving forward and starting from the stern of the superstructure the detail work was carried out. Bridging right across the beam of the tug from side to side and immediately above the stern of the engine-room casing was fitted a large towing bow, similar to that already fitted to the main deck of the model at the stern. This bow was made in the same way as the first but was attached to the engine-room casing only, using the cast brackets provided. As it is detachable along with the superstructure it needed to be made with care and substantial enough to withstand some handling. This is another reason why I decided to fit the switch gear and charging sockets under cases on the deck to avoid repeated removal of the top at the lake-side. The finished tow bow was painted black once it was fitted.

Just forward of the back of the engine-room casing were located two hatches for access to the space below. These were of white metal and were glued down, after painting, using superglue. The skylights already mentioned were fitted next, followed by three small tow bows formed from brass rod and fitted into brackets of cast white metal on either side of the engine-room casing. A fourth tow bow made from white metal parts and painted black was fitted at the forward end of the casing. On each side of the casing there were handrails formed from cast supports and wire and these completed the work on the engine-room casing.

The coal bunker was completed by building up the hatch surround from the cast and rivet detailed parts provided, followed by fitting the false floor needed to carry the coal. The interior was painted black by brush, once more using acrylic paint, and when it was thoroughly dry, coal was carefully broken into very small pieces and secured in the open area with thinned-down PVA glue. The hatch covers were fitted and the three that would be used to cover the area where the coal was visible were glued randomly over the correctly fitted covers. The hatch covers were made from thin plywood, stained with spirit stain and fitted with the cast handles provided in the kit. It should be noted that some of the cast parts in this kit are very small and need to be handled and stored with care - they are easily lost in the usual clutter of the work bench.

To complete the stern area of the superstructure the tow hook assembly was constructed from the cast parts and painted, as recommended, first with white primer and then in black. The hook and its latch arrangement is assembled so that it works correctly but it could be glued into a solid unit if so required. In its cast form it is not really strong enough to be used functionally so that tug-towing enthusiasts must find an alternative place on the stern of the model to which to attach a tow rope. The tow hook assembly, as built from the kit parts, is a very accurate reproduction of a Liverpool pattern towing hook. The other popular towing hook pattern is illustrated in one of the sketches.

Chapter 6   Small tugs, drive gear and towing

There are numerous small tugs used in handling barges and small craft within the confines of rivers and canals throughout the world. Many such tugs are specifically designed to provide the service for which they are used. Not often found in the UK, but in frequent use on the large continental and American rivers, are pusher tugs. These are built to propel their barges from astern and have a heavy framework of timber and/or steel at the bow to do this work. The barges are lashed together, usually in pairs abeam, and connected to the tug so that it can push and steer the whole set up or down river as required. To my knowledge there are no kits of such tugs yet available in the UK but quite a few enterprising modellers have built such units from scratch as can be seen from the photographs.

On the Thames for many years, the barge-handling tugs have been of the towing kind. In the early days of steam propulsion and coal firing, funnels and masts were arranged to be lowered to permit the vessel to pass under the various bridges. Today the more modern tugs have very low funnels that allow the tug to freely travel up or down river. The bridges upstream from Tower Bridge on the Thames are too low to allow normal ships to pass thus many ships unload onto barges downstream of the Pool of London and the cargoes are carried by barge and tug to their destination on the riverside further upstream. This traffic has, of course, declined over the years but there is still a small percentage of such to be seen by the keen observer. A very good example of a Thames river tug is *Riverman*, produced in kit form by Caldercraft (see Appendix 1) and this kit makes up into an attractive working model. *Riverman* is a single screw, conventionally driven tug whereas many of the modern tugs to be found on rivers are driven either by Schottel or Voith Schneider units, and often with two or more units to give good manoeuvrability.

Recently it has been noticed that tugs in the USA are increasingly being built with inboard/out-board drives such as the Schottel or azimuth system with, in some instances, the drive units being forward of the accommodation blocks so that they pull the vessel as distinct from pushing. These types of drives are becoming increasingly popular with tug designers as they permit the tug to exert its bollard pull in almost any direction and thus can handle the large vessels much more easily. Graupner, Robbe and Marx Luder from Germany all produce Schottel drive units in a small range of sizes but no maker, at this time, produces a Voith Schneider unit. The complexity of the Voith Schneider drive means that the model builder really must have access to, and ability to use, a small lathe to make such drives for a model. Graupner did, for a short while some years ago, make a Voith Schneider unit but these are no longer made and are becoming very rare indeed - if you do locate one then it is a valuable prize.

The handling of barges in both tidal and confined waterways is quite a skill learned by experience over the years of working on the tug. It is probable that the pusher tug handles its barges more easily than the towing tug as, in effect, the closely coupled barges and tug become a single, almost conventional ship. The tug that is towing a train of barges has to consider how they can be stopped as well as how they can be steered. Quick stops by the tug will cause the barges to overrun the tug with catastrophic results. Over the years it has not been unknown for tugs to be overrun by their tows and to be sunk or overturned with some loss of life. Good handling and quick reactions from the tug master will generally avoid such problems but it is usually anticipation of the problem before it occurs that wins the day. To watch a tug master draw his barge(s) alongside a ship for loading is to see for oneself how skilful a good master can be. The usual complement for such tugs is three - master, engineman and deckhand with the addition sometimes of a boy - and this crew with complete confidence will manoeuvre the barge train competently. It is also usual for the train of barges

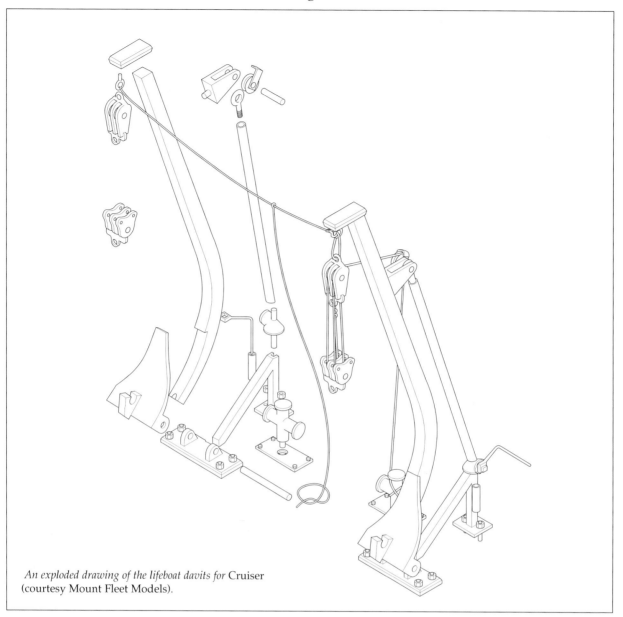

An exploded drawing of the lifeboat davits for Cruiser
(courtesy Mount Fleet Models).

to have at least one man aboard to assist with steering, to shorten the tow rope etc., as necessary.

Successful towing in miniature frequently depends upon how the tow is 'roped up'. It is a mistake to have the leading tug use a long tow rope when negotiating a tight regatta course as there will be a delayed reaction when turning; it is much more sensible to use a short hawser so that the turns are sharp and accurate. Similarly it is best to 'rope' the stern tug stern on to the tow so that maximum thrust can be used to brake and slow the tow down. Practice on the part of the tug-towing team will soon avoid any possibility of the tow overrunning the leading tug. Tugs handling large ships in confined waters such as a river or canal will invariably couple up close to the tow so that they can turn the tow accurately and sensibly ensure that the tow remains within the navigable parts of the river. Conversely, if the tow is ocean-going and the tug is hauling for a

long distance then the tow hawser will usually be very long - up to even half a mile.

One danger to watch for and avoid is the possibility of the tug becoming beam on to the tow so that the tug is drawn sideways and sometimes capsized - this can happen when working with models just as easily as in full-size practice and prompt action by the tug master is needed to turn the tug quickly enough to avoid the danger. For this and other reasons the model tug to be used in towing competitions needs to have adequate power, not only to haul the tow but to easily move out of danger when necessary. When fitting a towing rope between a model tug and a tow always ensure that it is of cord and not of wire. Wire has little elasticity and can cause serious problems by its stiffness whereas cord has a degree of elasticity and can act as a spring when taking up the weight of the tow. A hasty snatch on the towing hook or bollard can cause undue strain on it if the weight

The after end of the superstructure on Cruiser *showing the deck wings with curtain plates under the lifeboat.*

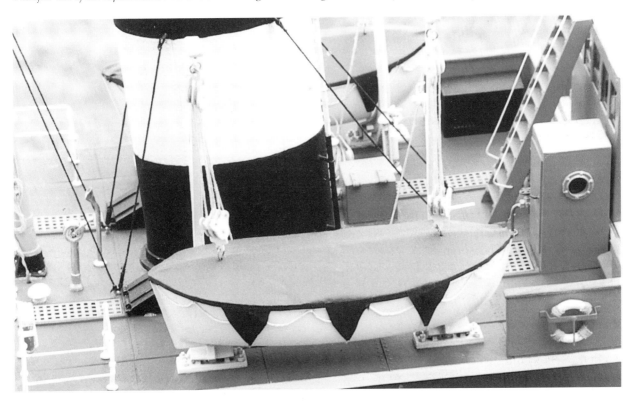

Further detail of the boat deck on Cruiser *showing the lifeboat and falls etc.*

of the tow is applied too quickly - always take up the slack of the tow rope slowly when moving a tow that is dead in the water. It is not unknown for the tow hook of a model to be pulled clean out of the model by a hasty move on the part of

the tug. Tugs, when handling full-size ships, do not proceed quickly but move with care and slowly so that there is little chance of the tow taking control and running away by its sheer weight. A 40,000-ton deadweight tanker takes a great deal

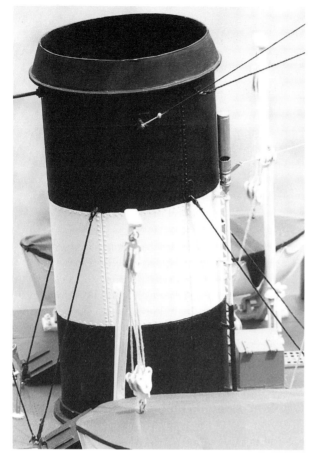

The funnel detail on Cruiser. *Note the steam whistle and tops of davits. Almost all funnels were secured with guy ropes to the deck.*

A pusher tug built by Peter Backhouse from Goole on Humberside.

Riverman - *a model of a Thames river tug from the Caldercraft range* (photo courtesy Jotika).

Wyeforce - *a model built by Peter Chappell from a Model Slipway kit illustrating the number of tyres fitted round the hull.*

of stopping once it has started to move and as they don't have brakes, it gets worse as the tow gets bigger.

Small tugs used mainly for barge handling or for harbour duty have substantial belts of timber or rubber-faced steel round their hulls to protect them from damage when running alongside or when pushing or pulling their tows. Huge rope fenders fastened round the bow were common on many tugs and large lorry tyres are frequently used to protect the sides and stern of tugs in preference to the more expensive rope fenders of the Turk's head pattern used on the more elegant small steamers and yachts. Most good model ship shops stock both rope pattern fenders and miniature tyres, while some of the makers of model tug kits include such items as fenders or tyres in their kits - *Wyeforce* by Model Slipway is one such kit including tyres.

Within magazines such as Ships Monthly and Sea Breezes can be found articles and photographs relating to full-size tugs; both magazines frequently list and describe new building of tugs and there are many informative articles relative to tugs and their work to be found in the back numbers. Much valuable information can be found by reading

through such publications and some of the larger central libraries carry copies of these magazines for researchers' use on the premises. The keen model tug man/woman will be well advised to spend time in such libraries seeking data on tugs and to look into the maritime museums at many ports for further data. Good models can only be built, even from kits, by researching into the vessel's background where possible.

Cruiser - boat deck, davits and bridge

Continuing with *Cruiser*, the boat deck was next tackled. The funnel having been painted and fitted

The Thames tug Sandra *clearly showing the large cowl ventilators used to supply air to, or extract air from, the engine-room according to the direction the cowls were facing.*

with the cast rings to carry the steam and whistle pipes, the guy attachment rings and the rungs for the access ladder, was next mounted over the previously cut oval hole in the deck. Four cast metal angle brackets are provided in the kit to assist in securing the funnel to the deck and these, together with a substantial fillet of car body filler (P 38), were used to hold the funnel in place. This joint is, in fact, so strong that the whole superstructure can be lifted from the model using the funnel as a handle. The whistle pipe was next fitted and glued in place followed by the steam valve box on the port side from which the exhaust steam pipe from the boiler safety valve exits. The steam pipe was connected to the box and to the funnel, both steam and whistle pipes were painted to match the funnel colours once the adhesive had dried.

Aft of the funnel on both port and starboard sides were fitted the ventilators over the gratings. These ventilators of the forced fan type obviously replaced what would have been cowl vents in earlier days and the castings were assembled and painted black before being fitted. The gratings which run on both sides of the boat deck were painted grey and glued in the locating slots. A telegraph, voice pipe and mushroom vent were next installed aft of the funnel together with the base for the main mast. The guy ropes supporting

the funnel were next fitted, these were made from the black rigging cord supplied and were each run through the block of beeswax provided to lay the loose fibres before being attached to the funnel and the deck rings.

The davits for the boats had been made some time before while waiting for the hull paintwork to dry out and they were next installed on either side of the funnel. The sketch and photographs show these clearly - they are a kit in themselves. They were glued down with 5-minute epoxy but also bolted through the deck using small 6 BA bolts and nuts. Although the davits are quite substantial being made from the white metal castings I felt that additional security was needed where the weight tended to draw the units over towards the sides of the model. The staghorn bollards were fitted at this time but the lifeboats and their falls were left off until all the work on the model was about finished.

Forward of the funnel and against the after part of the navigating bridge deck were next located and fitted two water tanks complete with pipework and valves. These valves were quite wonderfully cast in white metal with separate handwheels and they clipped over the brass rod used to simulate the pipes quite neatly; once painted and installed they look the part particularly well. To starboard of the tanks was fitted the companion with its portlights and door obviously leading to the accommodation below, and then the rails on either side were made from thin ply over 2mm x 2mm square stripwood, primed and finally painted with the same colour as the superstructure before the top rail of 2mm thick mahogany was fitted. Mahogany top rails were not specified in the kit or the instructions but were fitted to give the model a degree of luxury - the modeller's licence coming to the fore in preference to accuracy. They do look good though.

To complete this area of the model the two ball stanchions provided were mounted on a block of scrap balsa and painted white before being located loosely on the stern of the boat deck. Rails of the wire provided were next very carefully bent to fit round the deck and to form the handrails of the ladders at the stern. When each section of wire was correct the stanchions were threaded on and then glued firmly into the holes pre-drilled in the deck. The wires were also glued to the stanchions using superglue and the whole assembly left to cure overnight before being painted white in situ. Usually I tend to make up my handrails and stanchions off the model and to paint them before fitting but in this case it was not possible as the wire used was a loose fit in the holes which had been cast into the stanchions. This was not a fault as the finished rails are as good as any previously made off a model.

Attached to the sides of the forward solid rails and to the stern rails are four liferings. These were beautifully cast with detailed rope lashings cast into them, painted red and white and allowed to dry. The brackets to carry the liferings were made from thin strips of nickel silver left from etched sheets used on an earlier model. The strips were bent to shape and glued firmly to the model where necessary once they had been suitably painted, after which the liferings were put in place and tacked with superglue. Apart from the installation of the mainmast and the boats this completed the boat deck area.

Chapter 7   Model drive equipment

The question of what drive equipment to fit is one often asked by the novice or newcomer to the model ship scene. The vast majority of model shipbuilders fit direct current electric motors, batteries and radio control equipment and this is a perfectly satisfactory way to go. However, there are an increasing number of modellers opting to fit steam plants to models that depict steam outline vessels and there is an ever-increasing range of small steam outfits being produced in the UK and overseas at very reasonable prices. Both methods of driving the model tug are detailed here.

Electric motor drive is probably the cheapest and easiest drive system for the novice builder to consider as, with reasonable care and attention such a system will give few problems. As has been stated before, always buy the very best that you can afford as, usually, the higher priced motor will give less trouble in service than the cheaper one. The size of motor or motors that need to be fitted to a given model is often a source of problems and there is no really simple answer. If you were to obtain the power of the full-size ship then it is possible to calculate the power of the model using the formula:

$$\frac{\text{Power full size}}{\text{Root of scale to the power 7}}$$

Scale being taken as say 1:50 would give the formula:

$$\frac{\text{Power full size}}{\sqrt{50^7}}$$

This calculation is difficult and open to some question so that, in general, the size of the drive motor should be decided in consultation with the makers of the kit, or on the advice of a fellow boat club member or friend who has successfully built a similar model.

What is important is the speed at which to drive the propeller when the model is running at full throttle. All modern ships, whether driven by oil

engines or steam turbines, drive through gearboxes to reduce their economical revolutions to the speed needed for the propeller design. Except for small propellers such as may be fitted to fishing boats and small launches, marine propellers revolve in the speed range of 75 to 300 revolutions per minute on full-size vessels. These speeds, when converted to scale, give revs of 750 to 1500 per minute. Most electric drive motors have free-running speeds in excess of 8000 rpm which is much too fast for direct drive to a scale or near scale propeller. If a model is direct driven under these conditions all that happens is power wastage and cavitation at the propeller blades as the prop slips in the water and gives no real power.

It is necessary for the motor in the model to provide enough power to push the hull through the water at scale speed or a little more and to give adequate additional power to permit a tug, for example, to be used in towing a dead model of fair weight. A suitable gearbox between motor and propeller shaft will ensure that the required torque is obtained from the motor. A number of standard motors made specifically for the model ship have inbuilt gearboxes, while some, such as the Marx Luder range, include the provision of a planetary gearbox having four different ratios of 1:3, 1:4, 1:5 and 1:6 which can be selected by the modeller from the segments supplied. Others in the same range have gears built into one end of the motor casing so that either direct drive or drive through the gears can be selected.

Whichever motor is selected, it is essential to couple this to the propeller shaft using a flexible coupling and there are a number of good couplings on the market. The propeller shaft, coupling and motor must be mounted exactly in line one with the other for a trouble-free and friction-reduced drive. If the motor cannot be connected in line with the propeller shaft then a double coupling will be needed and used, preferably with the misalignment kept to the absolute mini-

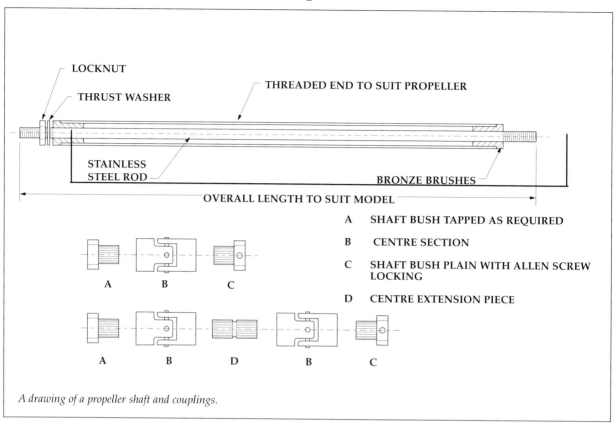

LOCKNUT

THRUST WASHER

THREADED END TO SUIT PROPELLER

STAINLESS
STEEL ROD

BRONZE BRUSHES

OVERALL LENGTH TO SUIT MODEL

A   SHAFT BUSH TAPPED AS REQUIRED

B   CENTRE SECTION

C   SHAFT BUSH PLAIN WITH ALLEN SCREW LOCKING

D   CENTRE EXTENSION PIECE

A   B   C

A   B   D   B   C

A drawing of a propeller shaft and couplings.

mum. Suitable couplings are illustrated in the sketches and photographs.

The motor fitted to Cruiser is a Marx Luder Decaperm rated at 6 volts and driving the shaft through the inbuilt gearbox giving a 2.75:1 reduction. With the propeller provided in the kit the model runs at a little over scale speed and gave a bollard pull of 3.5 pounds on a spring balance. This is perfectly adequate for the model which turns the scales at 42 pounds weight and it is quite manoeuvrable, although less so when running astern. Almost all single screw ships, full size or models, are difficult to steer when running astern.

Cruiser - completion, radio controls etc.

To complete the installation in *Cruiser* a lead acid battery of the sealed pattern rated at 6 volts and 6 ampere hours is fitted coupled to the motor through a Bob's board of resistive foil with wiper type as shown in the pictures. The two-channel radio is by Futaba and the channels control (1) the rudder through a servo and (2) the motor speed and direction through the board, also servo driven. The aerial from the receiver is routed round the forward section of the deckhouse upstand just above deck level. The installation of radio controls, speed controller, rudder control etc. is well illustrated in the photographs and a wiring diagram for this model is given too. Note that the power feed to the main motor isolating switch is fitted with a fuse (5 amp) and that the

radio is fed from the secondary battery through the battery eliminator circuit built (BEC) into the radio receiver. The secondary battery feeds the navigation lights, the smoke units and the radio system comprising receiver and servos. Navigation lights are operated from a manual switch under the overhang of the boat deck on the starboard side and comprise mast head and stern white lights with green and red side lights. The smoke units, which are also of 6 volt size, are fitted into the false funnel illustrated and controlled by the push on/push off switch fixed close to the rudder servo. This switch is actuated only when the trim lever of the rudder servo is set hard over so that when the rudder is turned the switch operates either on or off, but with the trim in the normal mid position the switch is not worked. This system allows a third action from a simple two-channel radio and is quite effective. Two smoke units are fitted to give a fair amount of smoke and ensure that it is visible from a reasonable distance. The wiring of these auxiliary functions is also illustrated by a wiring diagram on page 48.

There are differing combinations of R/C controls that can be installed relative to the installation of motors and auxiliary features. Twin motors on a twin screw tug will benefit from independent drive through a three- or four-channel radio and separate speed controllers. Some radio outfits, as described later, can be fitted with a wide range of switching to connect to relays or servos to oper-

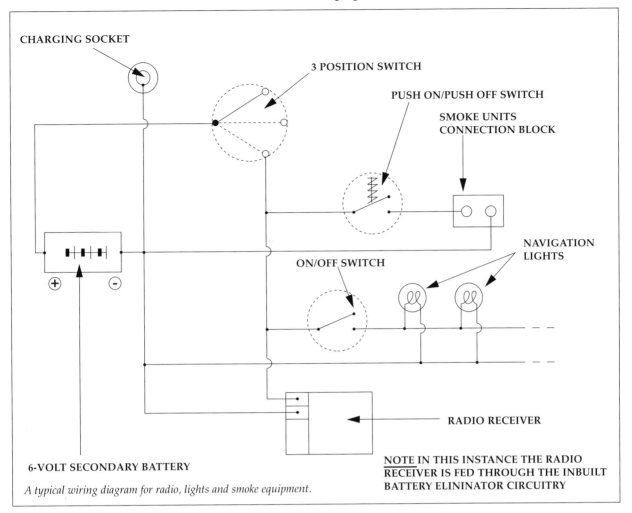

CHARGING SOCKET

3 POSITION SWITCH

PUSH ON/PUSH OFF SWITCH

SMOKE UNITS
CONNECTION BLOCK

NAVIGATION
LIGHTS

ON/OFF SWITCH

⊕   ⊖

RADIO RECEIVER

6-VOLT SECONDARY BATTERY

NOTE IN THIS INSTANCE THE RADIO
RECEIVER IS FED THROUGH THE INBUILT
BATTERY ELININATOR CIRCUITRY

A typical wiring diagram for radio, lights and smoke equipment.

ate various functions remotely, but it would be sensible for the novice modeller or the newcomer to the hobby to restrict activities to the simpler systems before moving on to the more sophisticated equipment.

Speed controllers require a degree of consideration. The simplest of all motor controls is the two-speed switch with direction operated from a simple switching arrangement from a servo and giving only two speeds ahead and one astern. Simple switches of this type can be found within the Robbe range. Next in simple form and very popular is the resistance board type over which a wiper system travels and is driven by a servo; this is the system used in *Cruiser*. More sophisticated, but becoming more and more popular, is the electronic speed controller which gives better speed control with a wider range of motor powers (the resistance board controls need to be sized to the motor loading) and can be bought in a very wide range of prices from low to quite expensive regardless of power range.

Today too, the electronic unit is often matched to the radio equipment by the radio maker and, obviously, a matched set of equipment from the same maker and supplier is almost certainly the

safer course to take. By far the largest manufacturer of radio equipment for the modeller is Futaba from Japan, followed by Sanwa and others, but a very fine range of radio equipment is produced in the UK by Fleet Control Systems (see Appendix 2). Further details will be given in a later chapter.

Moving to steam outfits there are a few points to take note of initially. Some kits are supplied having hulls moulded in ABS, Plura or other styrene-type plastics and such hulls cannot be used if a steam plant is to be fitted as heat from the plant will destroy the hull. Kits supplied with hulls of grp will generally be suitable for outfitting with steam drive but ensure that decks and upperworks of the model are of timber, plywood or similar material which is, to some degree, heat resisting. Decks and upperworks constructed of styrene sheet or material known as plasticard are not resistant to heat and will cause serious problems if used. Note too where the model can have ventilation built in as the steam outfit will need an adequate supply of air for combustion and cooling purposes. Some kit makers advocate that thin sheets of insulation material be used under decks to prevent heat from the plant causing problems with paintwork etc. Unless decks and deckhouses are located very close and almost touching the

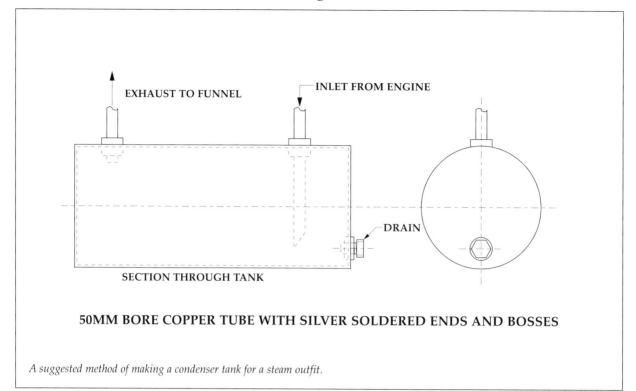

EXHAUST TO FUNNEL

INLET FROM ENGINE

DRAIN

SECTION THROUGH TANK

50MM BORE COPPER TUBE WITH SILVER SOLDERED ENDS AND BOSSES

A suggested method of making a condenser tank for a steam outfit.

boiler of the steam plant such insulation is really not needed if a good airflow is provided. Closely fitting upperworks round a boiler are better protected using reflective aluminium sheet glued to the undersides of the timber; heat is thus reflected away from the timber itself.

The modern steam outfits available today are built to conform to current regulations for the testing of pressure vessels. Used sensibly they are safe, although they do get very hot and will burn fingers if touched when in service. Most are fired by liquified petroleum gas (LPG) and the generally recommended gas is a mix of butane and propane in the proportions of 70% butane to 30% propane. The gas is supplied contained in suitable tanks and fed to the burner(s) through suitable valves of brass or bronze and copper pipes. Most manufacturers will also supply at extra cost rechargeable gas tanks which can be filled from the commercially produced containers using suitable adaptors. Such tanks and the boilers are pressure vessels and must be tested periodically to prescribed pressures for the needed insurance certification.

Model boat clubs throughout the UK and most of the world demand that only those steam-driven models that have valid test certificates for the steam plants and have valid insurance certification may sail on their waters. Steam outfits built by the model builder need also to be tested by an approved testing station before being placed in the model and on the water. Many model boat clubs have pressure testing facilities and suitably certificated testers to carry out boiler and tank testing.

Mabuchi 380 and 540 motors for 6 and 12 volts (photo courtesy Robbe Schluter UK).

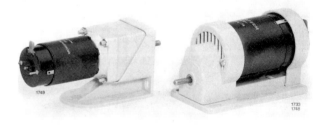

Marx Luder motors - Monoperm, Monoperm Super, Monoperm Super with pile gearbox and Decaperm. Monoperm generally for 6 volts with the Decaperm available for both 6 and 12 volts (photo courtesy Graupner).

The largest range of steam plants currently produced in the UK comes from Cheddar Models and smaller ranges are available from John Burrell Engineers and Stour Valley (see Appendix 2). Martin, Howes and Bayliss did make small steam outfits for their range of kits but now concentrate on kit manufacture and recommend the Cheddar range. The kit maker R M Marine does make some small kits utilising a small oscillating

Model drive equipment

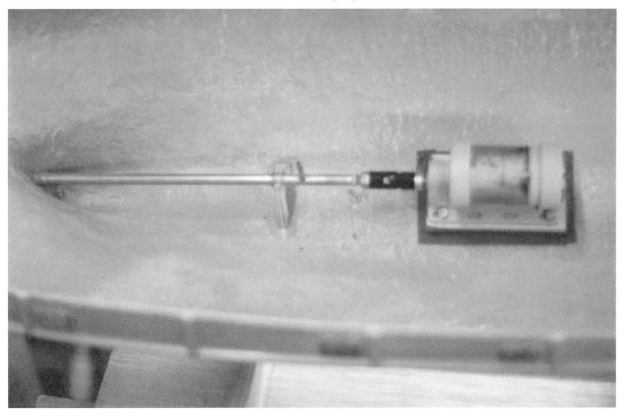

Decaperm motor fitted into Cruiser *and complete with Huco coupling and propeller shaft.*

Decaperm motor in Cruiser *with servo platform fitted over the propeller shaft and showing the closed-loop system from the servo to the rudder tiller.*

A range of brass propellers produced by E Radestock (photo courtesy E Radestock).

The funnel for Cruiser showing some of the detail work.

An overhead view of Cruiser's wheelhouse showing the binnacle, telegraph, wheel and voice pipes.

The wheelhouse for Cruiser fitted out and ready to be installed on the superstructure.

engine driven by steam from a boiler fired with methylated spirit and this spirit is also used for firing the boilers of the Japanese-made Saito steam outfits. Both of the latter steam outfits work with low steam pressures whereas the plants from Cheddar and Burrell work at pressures up to 80 psig.

The photographs illustrate steam plants of various types from UK makers and some show steam plants fitted into model ship hulls. In the same way as for electric motor drive, the alignment of

steam engine shaft, coupling and propeller shaft must be done carefully to prevent stress being placed upon the engine. Deviation from true alignment imposes loads on the drive equipment which can cause the engine to be overloaded and become uneconomical to run. Some of the photographs used to illustrate steam plants in hulls are not of either tugs or fishing vessels. On full-size ships fitted with reciprocating steam plants the propeller shaft drive system incorporated a thrust bearing unit, usually of Michel make or design, built to absorb the thrust of the propeller

The funnel fitted to Cruiser's *superstructure. Note the water tanks with pipework and valves which are almost hidden when the model is completed.*

The flying bridge fitted to Cruiser's *wheelhouse.*

and to ensure that no strain was placed upon the engine. The thrust was directed into the structure of the hull by the quite complex thrust bearing or block. It is sensible to ensure that no similar thrust is placed on the model steam plant by using shafts which will have very little detectable end float and which, thus, absorb the thrust from the propeller. Ships which use gearbox final drives usually have such thrust bearings built into the gearboxes and, in similar fashion, models using a gearbox between motor or engine and prop shaft will already have removed the thrust problem from the prime mover.

In general, model tugs of reasonable size lend themselves to easy installation of steam outfits -

tugs are generally beamy and of deep draught allowing boiler and engine to be sited correctly within the hull and beneath the superstructure. It is essential to see that space is available for the gas cylinder or spirit tank and also for the location of the condensate trapping tank that is needed. It is usually against regulations covering the sailing on public lakes and ponds to discharge oil products into the water and for this reason it is necessary to install a condense tank between the engine exhaust and the funnel or exhaust steam pipe. The steam feeding the engine of a model carries a small quantity of oil from the displacement lubricator to the cylinders to lubricate the cylinder walls and moving parts of the engine. Some of this oil is exhausted with the steam from the engine and is carried up with the exhaust to the atmosphere. If this exhaust steam is not trapped before being taken to the atmosphere then the oil will be deposited over the decks of the model and onto the water round the model. Some manufacturers include a condensate trapping tank as part of the steam outfit, others offer a condense tank as an extra at additional cost, in any event one such is needed to prevent the oil from reaching the model's decks and the lake waters. Periodically, of course, the condense tank needs to be drained of emulsified oil and water which must be disposed of safely away from the lake or pond. One sketch illustrates a basic condensate tank which, having no sealed or valved

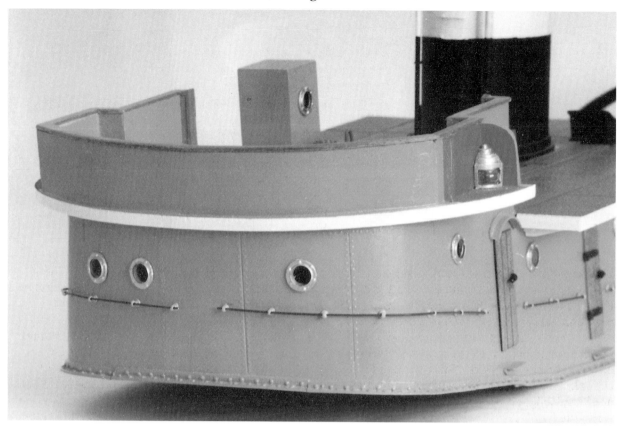

The forward view of the main superstructure for Cruiser. *Note the curtain plates in white.*

openings, is not subject to pressure from the exhaust steam and which does not need to be pressure tested.

The steam outfits of simple oscillating or slide valve pattern can often be operated from a two-channel radio system, but those that require separate operation of the reversing lever need the addition of a third channel. In all other aspects the installation of the radio equipment is similar to that required for electric drive. There is one very important aspect of radio control for steam ships and that is that steam and/or water and electrics DO NOT MIX. The wise modeller will install his radio control equipment in a water-resistant box as far from the steam plant as is possible and with the rods from the servos to the engine guided through the sides of the box through rubber bellows. Alternately the radio receiver and battery pack should be placed in a plastic bag with a small quantity of damp-absorbing crystals and the leads led through the neck of the bag and sealed with an elastic band. The drive servos should be fitted aft of the engine and behind a bulkhead slotted to accept the rods from the servos to the engine; in this way a degree of protection is given. Most servos are reasonably watertight and may safely be used in the way described. Always, but

always, once the sailing session is over, the model should be drained of all water and dried out before being stored between sessions. A hair drier will assist in ensuring that the servo and radio equipment is safe and, for further safety, the radio receiver and battery pack should be removed from the model and stored in a dry cool place.

The question of which size steam plant should be fitted to which size model is one best answered by the chosen steam plant maker. Almost all steam engines are able to be controlled from very slow to quite high speeds once they have been run in and they have the ability to provide good torque at low as well as high speeds. Under these circumstances it is rarely necessary to consider using a reduction gearbox unless, for example, the engine is to drive paddle wheels at slow speeds when at full throttle. The paddle wheel drive will probably need a reduction gear ratio as high as 40:1. With some small oscillating engines which run at high speed a reduction gear may be of benefit when the model is needed for regatta work round a steering course.

Steam engines are fun and great to use, but do take sensible precautions as laid down by the makers and keep small children at a reasonable distance.

Chapter 8   Tug details, lifeboats, davits etc.

The detail to be seen on a tug varies greatly with the period when it was built and with the duty for which it was intended. For example the small river and harbour tugs, whether steam- or motor-driven, rarely carried a lifeboat or davits but relied upon the use of a small dinghy usually to be found on the afterdeck. This boat was light enough to be manhandled over the side when needed. The larger tugs, coastal and ocean-going, were fitted with davits and carried lifeboats which complied with Board of Trade requirements. Smaller coastal tugs often only carried one boat whereas the larger vessels were fitted with two. All seemed also to carry a dinghy and most had a small derrick slung from the main mast which could be used to sling the dinghy into the water or to recover it. Almost always, in days past, tugs were secured to buoys in the river or harbour when not in use. They rarely berthed alongside a quay and the crews were ferried ashore in the dinghy or workboat. Berthing alongside a quay was more expensive than tying up to buoys, and the buoys were often solely used by the tugs of a given owner.

Various types of davits were fitted to tugs over the years, the earliest being fitted with radial davits and later ships fitted with later pattern davits as shown in the drawings and photographs. The most modern of salvage tugs all carry rigid semi-inflatable boats and liferafts in canisters to supplement the lifeboats. It is important for the modeller to spend time researching into the question of davits for a particular model and to ensure that the correct rope blocks (falls) are fitted. Some of the earlier davits were fitted with only simple triple sheave blocks and the lifeboats were swung out manually, later davits were designed to swing the boat out using a form of pivots and screws under control of a simple to use handle. Even later davits could be controlled electrically or hydraulically. All lifeboat falls, however, are arranged for manual operation. One or two of the photographs show the falls fitted to the model of *Cruiser* with

the anti-tilt blocks on the lower end. All davits must also be capable of manual operation in the event of failure of services on the ship.

Lifeboats form a highly visible part of the model ship be it tug, fishing boat, cargo ship or cruise liner. Early lifeboats were usually clinker-built from timber and were arranged for pulling with oars in rowlocks. Later these timber boats were fitted with buoyancy tanks fore and aft and sometimes under the thwarts (seats). In more recent times lifeboats have been built of steel and of aluminium but the latest boats are almost entirely of grp construction. Frequently a tug will carry a lifeboat that has a diesel engine installed as this can be used to transport personnel - a salvage or ocean-going tug will almost certainly have one such lifeboat. There are regulations laid down by the classification societies and, in the UK, by the Board of Trade, covering lifeboats, their construction and outfitting relative to their duty. The modeller needs to consult reference books and shipyard drawings to ensure that the correct lifeboats are fitted.

Building model lifeboats can be rewarding and there are a number of books that describe in detail how such models can be made; generally the kit maker will have included lifeboat shells in the kit for the modeller to complete and fit. Most lifeboats are secured in shaped mounts beneath the davits and fitted with tarpaulin covers tied in place over a beam fitted between the ends of the boat to allow water to run off easily. This does allow the model to be finished without the need to fit thwarts and interior detail as would be needed if the tarpaulin cover was omitted. However, all lifeboats do have grab ropes fitted all round the hull and, even if a cover is fitted, such grab ropes will remain visible. They can be seen clearly in the pictures of *Cruiser*. Grab ropes are best fashioned from twisted strands of fine copper wire in preference to cord as the strands can be curved to shape and glued without any problems. The cord sup-

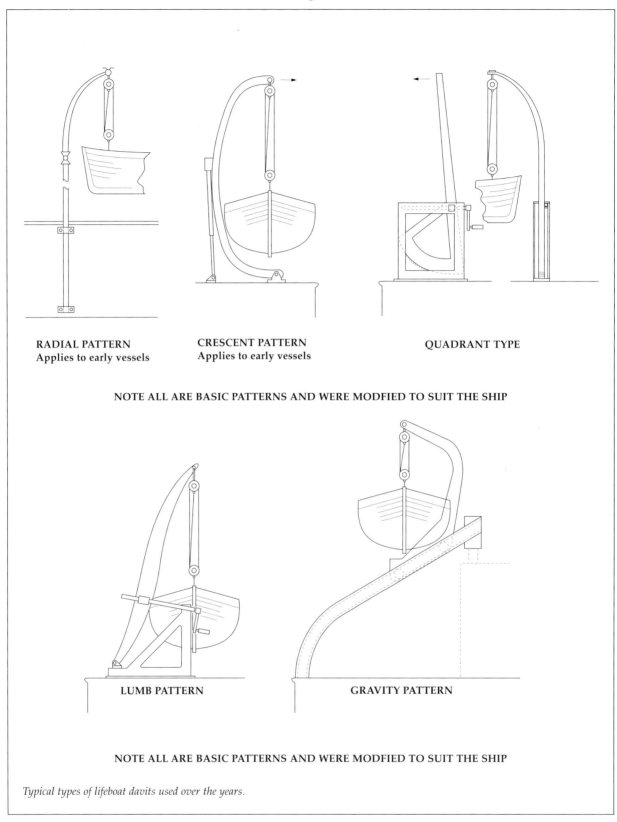

RADIAL PATTERN
Applies to early vessels

CRESCENT PATTERN
Applies to early vessels

QUADRANT TYPE

NOTE ALL ARE BASIC PATTERNS AND WERE MODFIED TO SUIT THE SHIP

LUMB PATTERN

GRAVITY PATTERN

NOTE ALL ARE BASIC PATTERNS AND WERE MODFIED TO SUIT THE SHIP

Typical types of lifeboat davits used over the years.

plied with most kits or purchased at the local model shop does not easily stay where it is intended. Before attaching a cover to a model lifeboat the finish paintwork needed should be done. The covers on the boats of *Cruiser* were made from heat-shrink film used by model aircraft builders to cover wings and fuselages of flying models. It is of plastic and can be attached to the model with heat from a domestic iron, and once in place, gentle heat from a hair drier or paint stripper used carefully will shrink and tension the covering. The material is available in various colours from good model shops and it is simple and clean to use. Many kits do not include material for simulating tarpaulin lifeboat covers and in the past I have used tissue paper tensioned by painting over with cellulose dope and colouring later - heat-shrink film is far superior.

Tug details, lifeboats, davits, etc.

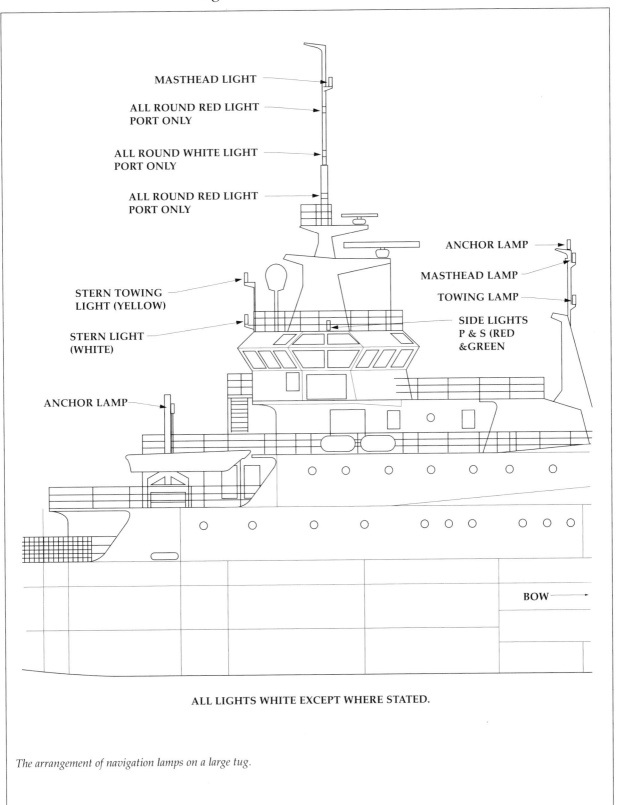

MASTHEAD LIGHT

ALL ROUND RED LIGHT
PORT ONLY

ALL ROUND WHITE LIGHT
PORT ONLY

ALL ROUND RED LIGHT
PORT ONLY

ANCHOR LAMP

MASTHEAD LAMP

TOWING LAMP

STERN TOWING
LIGHT (YELLOW)

SIDE LIGHTS
P & S (RED
&GREEN

STERN LIGHT
(WHITE)

ANCHOR LAMP

BOW

ALL LIGHTS WHITE EXCEPT WHERE STATED.

The arrangement of navigation lamps on a large tug.

For those lifeboats that are to be shown uncovered then it is important for the builder to detail the interior very carefully. As stated earlier, models are viewed mainly from above so that detail inside a lifeboat will be very visible. The clinker-built timber boat shows the planking of the hull clearly on the inside with the addition of the ribs, supports, thwarts etc. They were usually well varnished internally but painted externally and gen-erally white. Later boats of metal or grp construction show a painted interior with thwarts, bouyancy tanks and possibly an engine casing. Care is needed to get these interiors accurate and to scale - nothing looks worse than an out-of-scale fitting on a small model. Over the years there have been a number of first-class articles with illustrations published in the model magazines and a visit to the library should produce at least

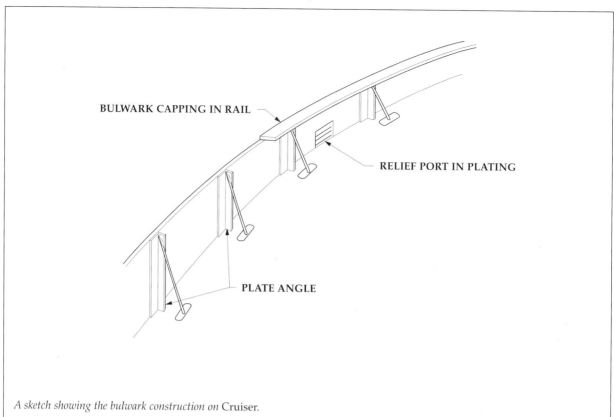

BULWARK CAPPING IN RAIL

RELIEF PORT IN PLATING

PLATE ANGLE

A sketch showing the bulwark construction on Cruiser.

one book giving comprehensive details of the various types of full-size boat. A Ship Model Maker's Manual by John Bowen gives excellent information on many lifeboat types and details of BoT standard sizes for lifeboats. Regretfully this book is now out of print, as is Model Open Boats by Ewart C Freeston which gives good detail on how to construct model open boats and lifeboats. Again, hopefully, your local public library should be able to assist and find a copy - odd copies do sometimes turn up in the large second-hand bookshops.

When reaching the final stages of building the model tug, or for that matter any model ship, check all the detail to be fitted and needed very carefully. It is best to make a list of what is required for fitting on the visible decks. I start at the bows and work back through the model to the stern, listing all visible fittings and their respective locations. Following this the preparation of such fittings can be checked, they can be assembled and painted and, once quite dry, they can be glued in place. Working in this manner it will be rare to find that a fitting has been overlooked. Preparing such a fittings list in the early days of construction will allow some of the fittings to be made and painted well in advance. They can be made during those periods of time when waiting for paint to dry or adhesives to cure and then can be painted and stored ready for use when the time comes.

At this point too, time will need to be spent upon the masts and rigging. All tugs, even the most

A single cylinder steam engine and boiler fitted into an all-wood model of the US tug Seguin.

A steam plant by Cheddar Models fitted into a model side fishing trawler.

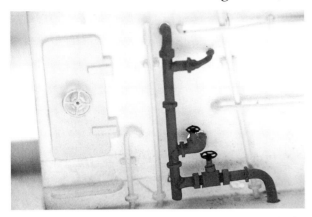

Detail of the fine pipework on a model support ship at a scale of 1:50. Note that the door in the picture is only 38mm high.

The fine detail on the main mast of Cruiser.

ship's supplies in an emergency in addition to the normal mains operated set. Such lights today are usually mounted in pairs with the battery operated lamp in the same casing as the mains unit, one set above the other - see the drawings with this chapter. The model builder needs to research the question of his model's lights carefully relative to the date of the full-size ship and the type of lights that would be fitted.

Details of how tugs were, and are, roped up to their tows have already been given but in recent months there have been a number of articles in the magazine Ships Monthly which have provided much information and a number of very good photographs of tugs in service over a period of time. How the tugs illustrated in this magazine are used is well shown in the fine pictures and seeking out such journals will be of value to the model tug builder. Tug masters are experts in their own field of ship handling and the model tug builder should take every opportunity to see tugs at work. This will not be easy as there are very few tugs in service compared to the number that could be seen 20 years ago, but a few visits to large ports such as Southampton, Liverpool, Felixstowe and Dover etc. may well prove worthwhile. Perhaps your local model boat club could organise a visit to a tug owner and his fleet, such a visit would provide a wealth of data for the model tug man.

A number of specialist companies produce films of ships and tugs at work using archive film shot in the past. These companies generally advertise in the shipping press and it may be useful to seek such videos out. Research is one of the pleasant tasks facing the scale modeller but it can also be very frustrating awaiting replies when one is panting to get on with the job. It is also possible to see and photograph tugs handling the very large tankers at an oil refinery if you can scrounge a trip on a pleasure boat which passes such places or at a bulk cargo offloading facility such as the Isle of Grain in the Thames. Large container ports such as Felixstowe are usually off-limits to unauthorised personnel unless a pass can be obtained from the port authority - it may be worthwhile finding out whether passes can be obtained if a specific tug is known to be operating at such a port.

Cruiser - completion of detail work and flying bridge

Returning to *Cruiser*, the navigation and flying bridges were next completed. Here I had a slight problem in that the printed ply decks were incorrect. I was made aware of this by the makers and I

modern, sport some kinds of masts; some have only one while others have two. The earlier steam tugs generally had two masts with the radio receiver and transmitter aerials strung between them. The foremast generally carried the navigation lights which varied with the period in which the ship was in service, the latest tugs would be fitted with a real 'Christmas tree' of lights. The very early tugs had lights illuminated by oil (paraffin) or naptha, later they were electric but with standby oil and the latest are all electric but with the standby set being battery operated. All ships are required to carry a full set of navigation lights which are not dependent upon the main elected to make my own decks using the maker's decks as a guide and covering the plain ply with planking cut from fine grain 0.8mm birch ply. The ply planks were sanded on both edges after cutting and a black, permanent ink, felt-tipped pen was used to blacken each edge before the planks were cut and glued in place. Before planking the bridge it was assembled in accordance with the instructions, curtain plates were fitted round the front and sides and part of the stern edges and the whole assembly was sealed with sanding sealer. The wheelhouse was next constructed from the parts provided and outfitted with bench, cupboards etc. The whole outer surface was primed and painted to match the main deckhouse and the assembly was set aside to dry.

The ship's wheel, binnacle and telegraphs were next assembled and painted along with the tea cups provided for the chart table. The wheelhouse was then positioned on the bridge and its outline drawn out. With the wheelhouse removed, the bridge was planked with the birch ply strips and margin planks were fitted round the outer edges. Where the wheelhouse was to fit was left bare as were the outer edges where the bulwarks were to be fitted. The bulwarks were made from the 0.8mm plywood and 2mm x 2mm stripwood provided as shown in the accompanying sketches but, departing from the kit, the top rail of the bulwarks was made from 2.0mm thick mahogany found in stock. The bulwarks inside and out were painted brown to match the deckhouse and the curtain plating was painted white.

The binnacle, telegraph and ship's wheel were next fitted along with the grating for the helmsman to stand on and the floor area of the wheelhouse was painted green. Once the paint had dried the wheelhouse was glued in place, the rails for the sliding doors having been fitted first and the doors put in place. The internal details of the wheelhouse were next completed, a couple of pages from a magazine being reduced to scale size and glued to the bench along with the two tea cups (mugs). The glazing was fitted in strips to the inside walls using Humbrol Clearfix which, if left for 24 hours, gives a firm fixing for such material and the inside walls were painted light grey.

Beams that support the flying bridge run through the port and starboard side tops of the wheelhouse – 4mm x 4mm square stripwood was used for these beams and the slots in the wheelhouse walls were cut to suit. At the outer ends of these beams brackets of cast, white metal were fixed to carry the rods to support bridge ends from the bulwarks of the main bridge below. Once they were carefully measured and deemed to be correct the plywood

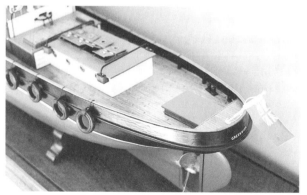

Three illustrations of the model Thames tug Sandra *built by Edward Heller in the USA. Note the fine detail achieved by this modeller* (photos courtesy Edward Heller).

shape of the flying bridge was glued to the beams with PVA and weighted down to stay flat until the adhesive cured. As for the navigation bridge, the flying bridge was planked with birch ply strips fitted inside margin planking. The locations for the rail stanchions were marked and drilled before the deck was sealed with sanding sealer and given a coat of matt varnish. Underside, the deck was painted white and when dry was glued in place over the wheelhouse. The binnacle, wheel, telegraphs and grating were assembled, painted and fixed in place using superglue. The bridge rail stanchions were painted white before being used and it should be noted that only the two lower rails are of solid wire, the top rail is of cord (to simulate the wire of the full-size ship). The rails were shaped up from the material provided and the stanchion and rails progressively glued down using superglue. At the aft side of the bridge the middle rails on either side of the access ladder bend down to form the handrails. The direction finding loop was made up, painted and fixed in place on the flying bridge and a model helmsman, assembled from the parts provided, was painted and attached to the wheel. Although a complete radar unit is supplied in the kit it was not fitted as I decided to depict the tug in its early days. Model aircraft covering was supplied from which to make the canvas screens for the flying bridge - this was very successful and can be seen in the photographs. It was attached to the stanchions using the tip of a clean 25 watt soldering iron to activate the adhesive in the material and this method worked well and first time too.

Cruiser - masts and rigging

A careful check of the model indicated that only the masts and associated rigging was needed to complete the building work. The masts were supplied as lengths of fine pine dowel and they had to be cut to length and sanded to the needed shape using the mast bands and fittings as guides. This is a somewhat lengthy job using various grades of sandpaper with the dowel being turned in the chuck of an electric drill. Care is needed to ensure that the taper is straight and not curving, and also to ensure that you change from coarse to fine paper before too much dowel is removed. At regular intervals the appropriate mast bands were tried on the dowel until the correct size was reached. The foremast was completed first, painted buff (mast colour) and fitted with all the necessary bands then laid aside while the main mast was made. Making the main mast was a little different as it is in two parts which need to match exactly where they fit the top section and in the twin supports. Once again the masts were sanded in the drill until they con-

formed to the required sizes of the fittings; they were then painted and assembled with fittings as per the drawings in the kit.

There were mast steps cast in white metal for each of the masts and these were fitted to the appropriate positions on the boat deck and bridge. Each mast was stepped, glued to the steps with 5-minute epoxy and held firmly until the epoxy set. It was necessary to sight the masts as they were fitted to ensure they did not lean to one side or the other and to hold them in place until the glue set. For complete safety the model was set aside overnight. The main (after) mast was rigged first being the simplest, the cord supplied in the kit was drawn through the supplied block of beeswax to lay the fibres before it was used and all knots securing the rigging were sealed with a drop of superglue.

The foremast is more complex as it carries the fixed navigation lights and the brackets for the standby oil lights. The top light of the foremast and the stern light on the main mast were fitted with 'grain of wheat' clear 6 volt bulbs with the cables being taped to the masts where necessary. All other lamps, save the port and starboard lamps on the bridge wings, do not work. The port lamp is, of course red and the starboard lamp is green and the four lamps are operated by a small slide switch concealed below the starboard forward davit. The oil lamps on the wire cable system were assembled and painted before being roped up to the bracket at the top of the mast and the rings let into the rail of the bridge bulwarks. Finally the chimney system from the crew's quarters was fitted up the front of the bridge and attached to the foremast with the appropriate brackets.

Careful examination of the photographs will show that the standing rigging is terminated at the masts in fine chain and at the decks to rings. This is a task that needs a gentle touch, slender masts of dowel can easily be pulled over if the rigging is tightened too much and yet such standing rigging is, and looks, incorrect if it is not fairly taut. Achieving the happy medium takes time and patience, the end result will fully justify the effort if all looks right. Happily all the rigging on *Cruiser*, except the two forestays, lifts off with the deckhouse assembly. The forestays were made with the cord supplied but the lower couple of inches were carried out in shirring elastic and small brass rings which hook the stays to the forward bollard. Shirring elastic holds the stays quite taut and is easily replaced if it stretches too much or snaps. To remove the deckhouse it is easy to unhook the forestays first.

Now, at last, it appeared that all the initial building work was complete, but was it? There were still some cast parts in the boxes, what had been missed? Easy - two of the crew had not been assembled and painted and there were a number of spare parts that had not been needed, supplied in case of breakages maybe. Double-checks showed only the crew figures were left and they were quickly assembled, painted and set on the stern. Basin trials next.

The domestic bath was called into use for the basin trials. The model was fitted out with the two lead acid batteries, the smaller one serving the lights, smoke units and receiver through a BEC system and the larger serving the motor. Radio controls were bench tested and fitted and finally the model was placed carefully in the water. It rode quite correctly upright without any list to either port or starboard but it was very high out of the water. Having been warned that the model needed a good deal of ballast I proceeded to place weights (blocks of marble from a trophy maker) in the hull until it sat close to the correct waterline. The model was then removed from the bath and the blocks were weighed - a total of close to 30 pounds was needed. Sheet lead such as is used by roofing contractors for flashing was next cut into small sheets and laid in the hull around and under the battery boxes, up the sides almost to deck level and as evenly as possible from bow to stern. The boat was then returned to the bath and further sheets added and secured with catalysed polyester resin until it lay to the waterline and truly vertically. Upon testing on the scales later it was found that it weighed in at a massive 42.5 pounds - a hernia-inflicting model unless handled carefully.

Tests on the water proved at first difficult, as the originally fitted electronic speed controller seemed to have a mind of its own; this was replaced by the old reliable Bob's board which has since proved more than adequate. *Cruiser* sails well at a little more than scale speed, she responds to the rudder well going ahead but less well running astern which is a normal response for a single screw ship, model or full size. Being quite large it is doubtful if she would be useful on a steering course of a regatta but that could be wrong as she does turn well. Duration with the 6 volt Decaperm and 6 volt 7.5 amp hour main drive battery is about 2.5 hours on one charge and this is more than enough for any regatta sailor.

The final conclusions are that it was a pleasure to build although very close to scratch-building in some cases, that it looks well when completed and that there were no serious snags. There were, as there are with anything, a few niggles but not enough to cause problems and the maker is at the end of a telephone and always willing to help when necessary. A very worthy project.

It follows that most of the tug kits offered today by the manufacturers listed herein take the same guidelines as those for *Cruiser*, but it is in the hands of the individual to select the tug best suited to him or her and to apply some of the advice that it is hoped has been provided here. Do, however, take care when purchasing your kit - whenever possible examine it thoroughly in the shop and if buying by mail order ensure that you can return it and get your money back if it is not to your requirements. As a general guide the more expensive kits are usually the most comprehensive and come with the best warranty - the cheaper kits can have snags and offer less in the way of guarantees.

Chapter 9   Model tug details and optional fittings

It will be noted that the model of *Cruiser*, as depicted in the photographs, has no rope fenders fitted at the bow or large tyres fastened round the perimeter of the hull for protection. In full-size practice large lorry tyres (used and not new) are suspended almost all round the hull of the tug and give a great deal of protection to the ship when it is in service pushing and handling large vessels. The kit of the tug *Wyeforce* contains about 36 such scale tyres to reproduce exactly the effect of the full-size ship which is festooned with tyres. *Cruiser* was built precisely from the kit and was not enhanced with any fittings which were not provided by the makers, thus it is shown bare of fenders and tyres; in the fullness of time such additional fittings will be added. It really would not be correct to depict a model tug on the water without such additional fittings and most good ship model shops can supply tyres and fenders both for bow and stern of models. Fenders of knitted cord feature in some model makers catalogues.

Model crews

Regretfully many model ships, not necessarily only tugs, are sailed today without a crew being visible at all. While many modern ships carry quite small crews, when they are underway crossing seas or oceans the ship can be under automatic pilot but some crew members will certainly be seen except in extreme weather conditions. Few kits offer the modeller crew figures as a standard within the box but *Cruiser* did have three crew members cast in white metal. These figures were in separate pieces which had to be glued together with the arms positioned, for example to hold the ship's wheel, and they had to be painted. They can be clearly seen in some of the pictures. There is no doubt that a few crew members going about the ship's business do lend a degree of realism to the finished ship. It is not enough just to scatter figures over the decks - they should be used sensibly and be seen to be doing a specific task such as steering, painting, coiling rope hawsers, washing

down the deck etc. The odd figure, sitting upon an upturned bucket, peeling potatoes or doing some such task is a good idea. Among the Caldercraft range of kits are some which include figures as a standard, one even includes the ship's dog.

Scale figures are available within the ranges of most kit manufacturers and they vary in size to suit the scales of the models within the respective ranges. Most figures are of cast white metal construction but some are of cast resin while others are of a cast plaster with wire reinforcement. Some are supplied ready dressed and painted and are thus of specific persons, others are supplied in parts and can be assembled and painted in various forms. The larger figures are sometimes supplied with cloth clothing or can be fitted with such clothing made to fit.

Protecting the model

Once the model is completed it is assumed that all the paintwork will have been done and an adequate drying-out period of time allowed. All models will, however, benefit from careful examination to ensure that no parts have been left unpainted or that some fittings have been forgotten or omitted. The greatest enemy of the modeller is dust; all models seem to collect dust as if it were going out of fashion. The best protection that can be given to the model is the provision of a case in which it can be kept between sailing sessions. Carry cases for models can be simply made from plywood or hardboard with square stripwood to reinforce the corners and with a thick plywood or MDF base on which the model, on its stand, can rest. The front of the carry case can be arranged to slide open to allow the model to be removed or installed and a typical wooden carry case is shown in the sketches. It is possible to buy sheets of clear styrene from which to make the front of the case and this will allow the model to be seen and thus the case can be used to display the model at the lakeside or at special events. This type of display/carry case is

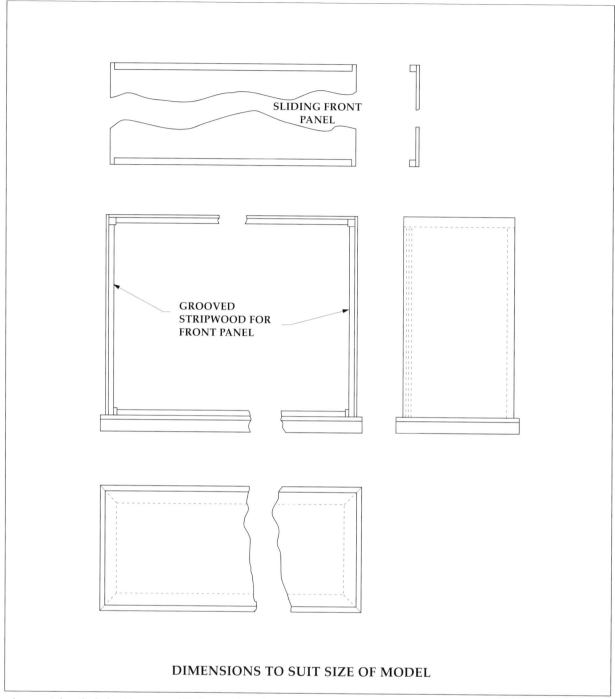

SLIDING FRONT PANEL

GROOVED STRIPWOOD FOR FRONT PANEL

DIMENSIONS TO SUIT SIZE OF MODEL

A suggested method of making a carry/display case for a ship model.

also of advantage at the pond when small boys or girls come to see the models - the model can be seen without being touched. Children seem to see more easily with their fingers than with their eyes and seem to have eyes on their fingertips which, unfortunately, all too frequently poke and cause some damage. Children should be encouraged to have interest in models but they should also be taught to treat them with care. Many young children show surprising skill at quite early ages when it comes to steering a model round a series of obstacles. They are, after all, the future members of the model club and builders of the next generation. Regretfully there are no apprentice

schools now to teach the crafts used in shipbuilding and it is only through models that children can learn of the fascination of model shipbuilding and sailing.

Fire monitors in miniature

Some model boat clubs today specialise in events which include tugs; they offer tug-towing regattas and stage demonstrations of sailing with tugs. Quite a lot of tug models are today fitted with fire monitors arranged to work under radio control and which spray streams of water in the same way as would a real tug. This is sometimes used

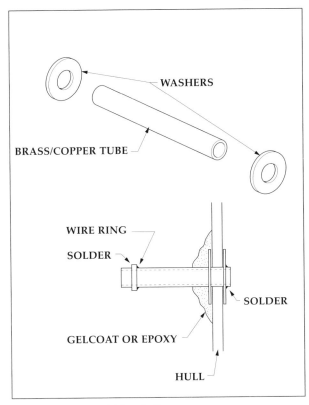

Skin fitting for a model boat hull.

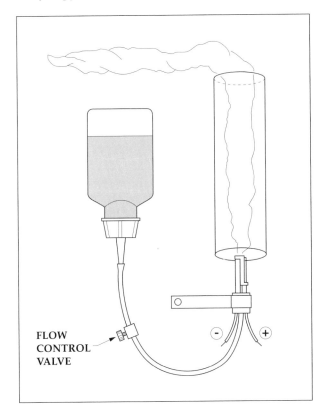

Smoke unit with feed tank (courtesy Graupner).

refinements need to be considered well in advance of building work. A number of manufacturers offer working model fire monitors as separate items for purchase and fitting but care should be taken to ensure that they are of the correct scale size or, at least, very close to it. It is a comparatively easy matter to make and fit a 'skin fitting' to the hull - a fitting projecting through the hull - to allow the pump of the fire monitor system to draw water from the pond and pump it through the monitor and just such a fitting is illustrated here. Care must be taken to ensure that the skin fitting and all water piping from the hull to the pump and from the pump to the monitor are watertight and that there are no leaks; it takes very little water to flood the model and the electrics with resultant costly repairs.

Cooling water outlets

All ships, including tugs, have their engines cooled by water circulating through the cooling jackets of the machinery. Such coolant water is evacuated through pipes which generally terminate just above the waterline. This water outpouring is easily seen in photographs of full-size ships and also when observing the real thing. In the same way as a fire monitor can be fed with water from a small pump so can the cooling outflow be made operative. It is a very simple task to make two skin fittings through the hull of the model, one below and one above the waterline; a small pump in the pipework between the two fittings will then draw water from the pond and pour it out of the upper fitting. The flow of water in this case needs to be quite slow and not the jet that is needed for the fire monitor. Suitable pumps can be found within the ranges of a number of makers but the small pumps used for car screen washers are also suitable and can sometimes be bought for very small sums from car accessory shops or scrapyards.

Operating smoke units

Apart from the fire monitors and water cooling outflows there are few features on the model tug that demand remote or automatic operation to aid realism. Tugs rarely use their anchors so that there is little point in installing what can be expensive windlasses to lower and lift the model anchor. While the towing winch can be made to operate and thus shorten or lengthen a tow hawser, when in service this is not an operation likely to be used even in a tug-towing demonstration or competition - there is little point in the expense. The steam tug did, and does, emit smoke when in service and the fitting of a smoke system will be an attraction if the model is electri-

to great effect to illustrate how a fire-fighting tug can control the fire on a burning model ship and give onlookers a real show of skill. The water system needed for the working fire monitor needs to be installed as the model is being built and, generally, before the main decks are laid so that such

Detail of a Graupner smoke unit built into a tank and showing the construction of a suitable funnel.

The stern of Cruiser *showing crew members supplied in kit form and suitably painted.*

cally driven. Steam will be exhausted by a steam plant if the model is so fitted so that a smoke system is not an item to consider for a steam-driven model. At the time of writing there does not seem to be a smoke system or oil that will generate black or dark brown smoke available commercially but the grey smoke looks very good issuing from a tall funnel.

The bridge on Cruiser *showing the helmsman and other detail.*

There are a number of smoke units on the market that have proved satisfactory in service for me, the larger and more expensive being that provided by Graupner and illustrated in the accompanying photographs. As can be seen this unit requires to be installed in a tank that can be filled to the required level with smoke oil. It also needs a 9 to 12 volt DC electricity supply to make it operate but it does generate a fair quantity of smoke when properly installed. It is also possible to use a small tank for the generator unit and to feed the tank from a larger supply in order to extend the duration of the smoke emission, see sketches.

The completed model of Cruiser *under test on a local canal basin.*

The smaller units produced by Seuthe are also very good and, in service, have proved to be robust and long lasting. The main disadvantage lies in the fact that they are small and that the smoke oil needs to be placed in the tube of the unit - these tubes are small and the duration of smoke generation is generally only a maximum of 20 minutes. Two such units of 6 volt rating were used in the funnel of *Cruiser* and worked particularly well, operation being by a push on/push off switch controlled from an extension arm to the rudder servo which depressed the switch when the rudder lever of the transmitter was put hard over and the centering lever was also thrown over. In the normal position the lever did not depress the switch when the rudder was hard over. This lever is illustrated in some of the pictures.

Radio control systems which were dealt with in Chapter 6 can be extended to permit the remote control of the additional functions described above and a multi-channel radio today can, quite often, have switchgear added to allow a suitable receiver in the model to operate switches which will switch on lights, pumps or other electrical controls for attractive additional effects while the model is underway on the pond. Such sophisticated extra radio fittings are not described here but details can be found by enquiring at most good model shops. Just as computers improve and become more sophisticated almost annually so does the modern radio control equipment, and most radio improvements or additions are detailed regularly in the model press.

The model magazines of today provide the ship modeller with a great deal of help and advice, much of which will prove of value. The adverts also assist in helping the reader to find the sources of those materials and fittings that the local model shop may not have the facilities to stock. It must be remembered that the local model shop does not usually cater for the model ship builder alone but quite often for the model car, train and aircraft enthusiast too, so it is impossible for it to carry everything the model ship-builder might need. Most good model shop owners will, however, order specific materials or parts if the cost justifies it and if the customer is prepared to wait for delivery. The shop specialising in model ships and advertising in the model press will generally offer a first-class mail order service and will usually be able to offer a wider range of fittings and kits. It is always wise to support the local model shop whenever possible as it is invariably able to supply the oft-needed items such a glue, cement, radio bits etc. and your support will help to keep the shop open and available for this service.

Chapter 10   Fishing vessel development

Within this section of the book will be found details of the building of a model fishing vessel which was constructed to be presented to the owner of the full-size ship when it was completed. The model and the full-size ship were built at the same time and many of the photographs used show the construction of the full-size ship. The model was built from scratch using a plank-on-frame hull in plywood with wooden decks but with styrene sheet being used for the superstructure and most of the remaining upperworks. The model was built for display purposes and therefore does not have any drive equipment. Before detailing any of this work the question of 'trawlers' as used in the title of the book must be defined. Just as 'Hoover' is synonymous with the

vacuum cleaner so 'trawler' is synonymous with the fishing vessel and, quite frequently, one can hear a herring drifter described as a trawler when it is not.

The first fishing vessels to be powered were those that originally were sailing ships, and as the steam engine was developed and installed in the early tugs it became apparent, to the more far-seeing fishermen, that powered craft could fish in more distant waters and, not being reliant upon the wind, could almost guarantee to get their catches into port at a given time. Although slow to start it took but a few years to see the end of the sailing smack as a commercial success however, many have been preserved and can be seen in

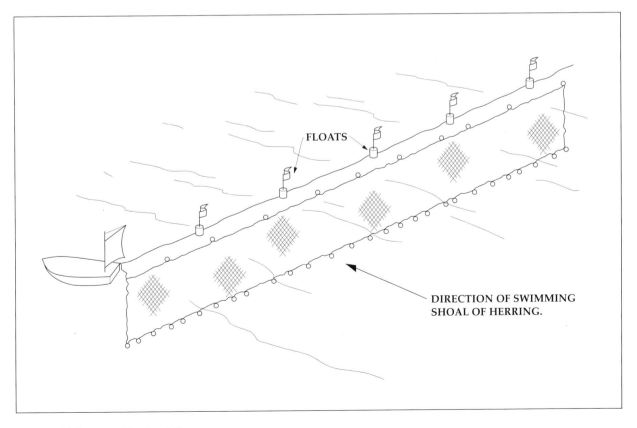

FLOATS

DIRECTION OF SWIMMING SHOAL OF HERRING.

The lay of drift nets and herring drifter.

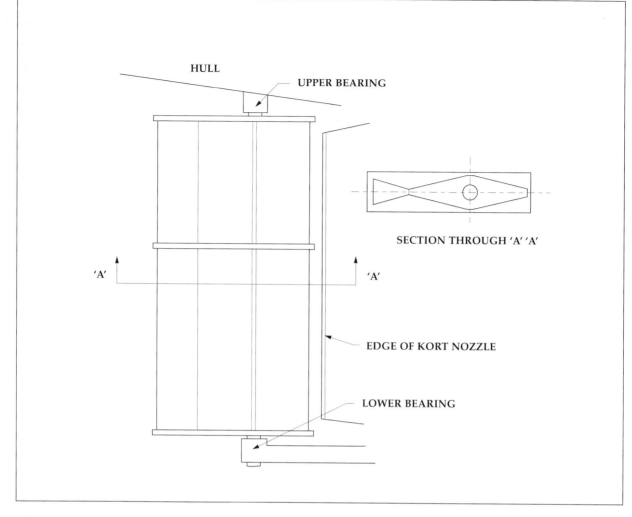

HULL

UPPER BEARING

SECTION THROUGH 'A' 'A'

'A' 'A'

EDGE OF KORT NOZZLE

LOWER BEARING

The arrangement of the rudder for Academus.

a number of places and taking part in special meets and races.

The herring drifter was one of the first ships to be successfully fitted with the steam engine, some using the simple compound two-cylinder plant and others using the triple expansion (three-cylinder) engine with virtually all being fitted with a cylindrical boiler, two or three furnaces and coal fired. Few herring drifters survived long enough to be converted to burning oil. Coal was carried in bunkers located on either side of the engine and boiler-room spaces and steam was generated usually at 100 to 150lb per square inch to feed the engine. In the earlier vessels the pressure of steam was much lower and the steam plant was quite crude, but ships built from the early 1900's were very much better and reliable. The herring drifters as illustrated in the photographs ranged from the north of Scotland to south of Yarmouth on the east coast each year following the shoals of herring and landing their catches at the nearest east coast port.

Model herring drifters in kit form are available from a number of suppliers, those of Caldercraft

A model of the herring drifter Formidable *underway on the lake. Built to scale 1:24 and outfitted with a steam plant and R/C controls (model built by the author).*

and Mountfleet Models being particularly accurate models of this pattern of ship. Drifters varied very little except for length and power, almost all were built in small yards located on the east coast of the UK and the vast majority were of wooden construction, but drifters made of steel and iron were built in quite large numbers between the two World Wars. In contrast to most other fishing ves-

A model of the modern stern trawler Glenrose 1 *originally fitted with an electric motor drive and R/C controls but subsequently placed in a display case for the vessel's owner.*

Keila - *a trawler/seiner from the Orkney Isles. This model was built for the owner complete with operating bow thruster, main drive motor and radio controls.*

Purse seine fishing boat Denebula *built for the owner for display only but with operating navigation lights.*

sels even of quite modern construction, the drifter was capable of a fairly high speed some reaching as much as 15 knots in service with even higher speeds up to 17 knots on trials. This speed was a decided advantage when driving for port and to reach there earlier than others and get the best

prices for the catch. The modeller interested in the herring drifter would be well advised to seek a copy of From Tree To Sea written and illustrated by Ted Frost (published by Terence Dalton). This volume describes and illustrates the building of a wooden herring drifter from the time the tree is cut down for the timber until the ship is taken out on trials. It is a masterpiece of descriptive literature with reference to wooden boat building and a great read.

No drifters, as far as can be ascertained, were ever fitted with refrigeration equipment and they had to carry large quantities of ice in which to pack the fish once caught. The herring is a 'pelagic' fish, swimming not too far from the surface of the sea and it was caught in drift nets in the manner illustrated in the sketches. The trawler fishes for cod and haddock etc., which are 'demersal' fish swimming close to the sea bottom. The design of the fishing vessel, particularly today, is dictated by the type of fish that it is to be used to catch. Such modern designs are intensively researched craft and they are outfitted with some very sophisticated seek-and-locate equipment.

Modern nets and winches are capable of collecting more fish in one sweep today than a drifter of the 1920s and 1930s could land in a week of intensive working - the bridge equipment is even able to tell the master the weight of the fish in the net before it is taken on board the vessel. Modern pelagic fishing boats do not bring their nets on board but pump the fish from the net into the ship once the net is drawn close to the ship's side. In a similar manner the fish, having been stored on the ship in chilled sea-water refrigeration spaces, are pumped ashore. Thus the handling of the catch is minimal and quick.

As previously stated, the modern fishing vessel is designed to suit the service in which it will be employed so there are many differing forms of fishing vessel around now compared to years ago. Within these next few chapters the various types of fishing vessel will be described, commencing with the earlier ships and going on to the largest of modern fishing vessels that today spend months at sea and travel great distances to put the large variety of fish on our menus. In the same way as the tug construction was described in the early chapters, so the building of a small scallop dredging fishing boat will be described.

Academus - hull and running gear

Academus, originally known to me only as Rix 151 of the Hepworth Shipyard at Paull on the Humber, is a small fishing vessel designed for scallop fishing from the Solway Firth port of Kirkudbright. The model was built with the hull of timber in a very similar manner to the full-size hull of steel. Many articles and books carry details of how to build the model ship's hull from timber in the plank-on-frame manner or in the bread-and-butter method so no words or space will be wasted in repeating such details. Suffice to say that the hull for the model of 151 was built from marine ply wood frames covered with ply planks and with the bow and stern fashioned from blocks of balsa as can be seen in some of the accompanying pictures. This hull was finished to a smooth surface using a rotary sanding machine followed by hand rubbing with very fine grades of finishing abrasive paper. This was to ensure that the hull would be of fine enough quality upon which to build a display model. More frequently my hulls are used as plugs from which to produce a mould in which further hulls can be moulded in grp. To ensure that the model hull would withstand the handling needed to build up a finished model, the outside was coated in catalysed polyester resin with a powder incorporated to give body. It was then sanded to a very fine finish and taken to the shipyard for comparison with the full-size ship. At this stage the model was about three weeks in advance of the full-size ship, but the opportunity was taken to examine the full-size unit, particularly the propeller shaft, Kort nozzle and rudder which were lying on the shop floor.

As will be seen the rudder was of an unusual shape and a sketch is provided to show this - it is believed that this shape gives very good steering characteristics particularly with small but beamy hulls. The beamy hull provides for good sea keeping in almost all weathers. In addition to getting copies of the general arrangement drawing, copies of drawings detailing the rudder, 'goalpost', forward mast and the wheelhouse were also obtained which allowed for masts and other features of the model to be prepared in advance while waiting for the full-size ship to catch up with the model work. Building a model following the real thing proved to be a most interesting and informative exercise.

As this model was for display purposes it was not necessary to make any arrangements for fitting drive equipment and radio gear, but it is at this stage of building that such arrangements must be

The side fishing trawler Kingston Peridot. *A model featured in Model Boats magazine over a number of issues. The model was originally steam-driven but was subsequently placed in a display cabinet for a prominent marine insurance company (model built by the author).*

made. The fitting of a suitable propeller shaft, Kort nozzle, propeller and coupling needs to be carried out with care. Lining up the drive, whether it be electric motor or steam engine, needs to be well done. A drive system that is even slightly out of line demands a double coupling and this should only be used to accommodate misalignment in one plane. Out-of-true drives place undue stress on the prime mover and waste power with the added hazard of overheating bearings and motors and causing expensive failure, usually on the lake as far from the side as possible or where it is difficult to effect easy recovery of the model. Extra time taken to avoid such faults is worth taking. When the drive is by electric motor it is relatively easy to check alignment by placing a sensitive ammeter in series with the supply and, while moving the motor on its mounting very slowly and carefully, the lowest reading on the meter will be found to be the correct location for the final fitting.

The question of what motor or steam plant to fit has been dealt with in Chapter 6 and it should be borne in mind that while the drive equipment found in the tug is needed to draw its tow and comes from the main engines, the towing of the trawl or nets in the fishing boat also comes from the main engines, the trawl and/or net winches are used to draw the nets in to the ship. The variety of winches that are available to the fishing master is huge, varying from very small cod-end winches to massive and powerful trawl and net haulers. Details of these will be found in subsequent chapters.

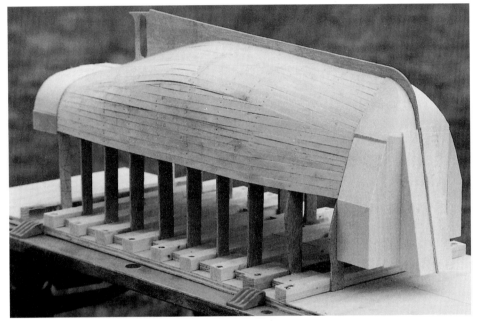

Three photographs illustrating the construction of the hull for the model of the scallop dredger Academus.

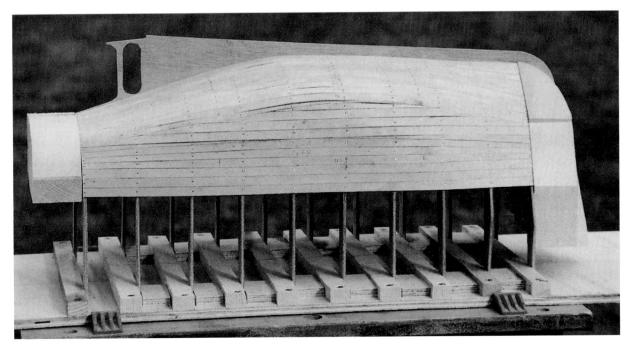

Chapter 11   The herring drifter and trawler

The starboard quarter view of the model of the herring drifter Formidable *to show the large cowl ventilators, navigation lights and backboard etc.*

The wheelhouse and superstructure on the model of the side fishing trawler Kingston Peridot *at a scale of 1:24.*

Almost everyone sees the herring drifter as the first steam-driven fishing vessel and, to some degree, this is correct. The earliest example dates back to 1880 although it wasn't until some 5 years later that the second appeared. Within a very short while the UK fleet of drifters ran to many hundreds and the method used by them to catch the herring led to the name 'drifter' being universally applied. These ships were very similar to the sailing drifters and few were built from accurate drawings, the majority being built initially from wood in many small yards mainly on the east

coasts of Scotland and England. The steel-hulled ships appeared first between the two World Wars and for many years the steel and wooden ships shared the seas around the coasts, following the shoals of herring as they travelled south and landing their catches at the nearest fishing port as they went.

Herring drifters laid their drift nets as shown in the sketches in a long line across the path of the fish and with the ship drifting to the end of the net using the sail hoisted at the mizzen mast. Always the nets would be drawn in by means of the steam capstan and the fish would be released from the nets as they came on board; the fish would be trapped by their gills and had to be shaken from the nets by hand. The fish were generally bulked in ponds in the fish-room but early in the season boxes and ice were carried to suit market forces. Most of the drifter's trips were of short duration, landing daily at the nearest port to ensure that the catch remained fresh when it was landed. As a boy before the last war I bought herring at the fish quay at North Shields on Tyneside at a cost of one old pence per twelve fish - these were then made into rollmops and proved to be very tasty.

The owners from the East Neuk of Fife successfully converted their drifters to long liners fishing for cod and halibut near the Faroes and in the northern part of the North Sea. The herring drifter was an attractive ship as can be seen in the many illustrations that abound in books of the period, the earliest carried very tall, slender funnels necessary to provide a good draught for the boiler furnaces and such funnels were likened to the cheap Woodbine cigarette popular during the period of these vessels. Later ships became more sophisticated and had the uptake from the boiler fitted inside an outer casing which insulated the funnel and helped to create better draught. Such outer funnels remained cool and could be more easily painted to suit the owner's individual taste.

The stern of the model Kingston Peridot illustrating the fine quality lifeboats from Quaycraft, davits and other detail.

Although there were, at one period, more than a thousand herring drifters in service, the passage of time brought science to the fishing industry and the herring drifter became outdated. Only one remains today, preserved in the port of Yarmouth. This is the *Lydia Eva* which is a steel-built ship but kept accurate in all detail.

Although powered a little earlier than drifter, the steam trawler joined the fishing fleets before the First World War. Designed once more closely to the sailing trawlers of the day they worked in cod and haddock fishing, bottom-feeding fish. The trawls used then, and even today, differ little save in the material used to make the nets. Fully described recently by me in articles appearing in the monthly magazine Model Boats (Nexus Special Interests), the nets are drawn almost across the sea bed with iron weights holding the bottom of the net close to the floor of the sea and with a series of floats holding the net open at the top. Trawl doors spread the sides of the net out and the fish are drawn into the small end of the net known as the cod end. This end of the net is closed by means of a rope so that, once the net is raised up over the deck of the ship, the end can be released and the fish dropped into 'ponds'. Ponds were sections of the working deck set into rectangular areas enclosed by boards in angle iron slots. The catch was sorted into these ponds before being gutted, cleaned and shot into the hold for packing in ice.

The earlier trawlers were mainly of the side fishing type i.e. 'side winders', shooting the trawl over the side of the ship, generally the starboard side but both sides could be used on most ships. Just forward of the wheelhouse or superstructure would be the trawl winch, a massive piece of machinery, steam-driven initially but later run by electric motor. In the case of the motor-driven winch the electric motor was usually housed beneath the wheelhouse under cover and protected from the elements. There seems to be but one trawler model kit available at the present time but there are at least two herring drifter kits from different makers (see Appendix 1). While the herring drifter seems always to have been a steam-driven vessel, the trawler lasted much longer and, at first had oil firing fitted in place of coal. Later ships were fitted with marine diesel engines. The herring drifters were never fitted with refrigeration equipment whereas the later trawlers were.

The steam or motor trawler and the herring drifter make attractive models and can be quite colourful. Almost all fishing boats were, and are, decorated to the taste of their owners and often in quite striking colours. You should, of course, be careful of making the model too gaudy or of overdoing the wear and tear factor when painting the finished model. If you are seeking a high placing in competition, you need to be wary of being heavy handed with both paint and weathering materials. There are a number of photographs illustrating the trawler *Kingston Peridot* and the herring drifter Formidable, both built by me - neither is lacking in colour but both are kept attractive. The trawler was built and outfitted initially with a steam plant which was later removed when the model was fit-

Academemus *showing the deck beams fitted to the hull and high foc'sle head.*

Academus *illustrating the large bilge keels and fine rubbing strakes.*

ted into a display case and subsequently placed on show in the offices of a marine insurance company. The herring drifter was first fitted with an electric motor and radio equipment but later fitted with a steam outfit and sold to the makers of the steam plant for demonstration purposes. Both models were built on grp hulls with timber decks and superstructures.

There were large fleets of such trawlers and herring drifters which fished mainly in waters reasonably close to their home ports; their ability to catch and land fish was restricted by the lack of refrigeration. The method of storing the fish was in pounds in the fish-room where the fish was shelved and packed in ice to ensure freshness. The steam trawler spent three weeks at sea under usual conditions, one week to reach the fishing grounds, one week to fish and one week to return. Fish caught early in the trip would deteriorate if not landed within two weeks. These constraints meant that crews needed to work particularly hard and fast in conditions that can only be described as horrendous. The steam trawler

Academus *showing the Kort nozzle and propeller together with the rudder unit.*

The stern of Academus *illustrating the rubbing strips formed from half round styrene strips.*

would carry a crew of thirty or more compared to the modern complement of 15 or less. Low bulwarks necessary for easy handling of the nets meant that it was all too easy to fall over the side and immersion in Arctic seas resulted in almost immediate death due to shock and the extreme cold of the sea.

The herring drifter fared little better - the North Sea can be, and is, a stormy one in winter and the drifter crews had no better protection than those of the trawlermen when working on deck. They sailed waters much closer to home but, in the herring season, worked continuously both at sea and in port when landing the catch. There was no shore leave in the herring season and as soon as one cargo was landed, supplies were loaded and bunkers were filled to allow the ship to sail with little or no delay. Time was money; in both cases crews were paid by a basic and very low wage supplemented by a share in the profit from the catch thus time ashore meant no cash and a poor catch landed late meant poor bonuses.

Although life sea-fishing today is much safer than it was by virtue of the design of the modern fishing vessel, the conditions still leave much to be desired and sailing in Arctic waters is hazardous in any ship. As will be seen in the following chapters, both fishing methods and fishing boats have benefited from modern designs and research. Among the early fishing boats that need to be mentioned are those that were fitted with marine diesel engines despite the fact that they were, and are, essentially sailing ships. The Scottish Fifie and Zulu and the east coast cobles and yawls have all been fitted with such engines very successfully. Fine seaworthy vessels, they are ideally suited to the type of inshore fishing for which they are used but sadly they too are slowly disappearing from our coasts. One kit maker recently added a Fifie to the range of kits available and it appears to be an attractive and accurate model when correctly assembled and painted.

Academus - decks, hatches and bulwarks

Continuing with Academus, once the hull was sanded to a satisfactory finish, deck beams of 4mm thick plywood were cut to fit across the hull. It should be noted that the sides of the hull of this model were trimmed accurately to main deck height and that the deck beams were fitted at the tops of the frames. For a model using a grp hull the deck supports running fore and aft round the hull must be fitted before the deck beams. The top of each deck beam was cut to the camber curve taken from the drawings provided, the method of calculating this curvature is given in Appendix 3. A total of five beams was fitted, set at equal intervals from bow to stern and this is suitable for a display model but not for a working model. Deck beams for the working scale model must be fitted and spaced to allow access to the inside of the hull through hatches or the removal of the superstructure, such access being needed for reaching the drive equipment, batteries etc. There are no hard and fast rules relating to fitting deck support beams on the working model but careful examination of the general arrangement drawings and forward planning will make the task possible. There will be some areas on ships that have long hatches where there is the need to fit deck beams in way of such hatches to hold the hull to its correct beam, and provided such beams are laid with sufficient space between them to allow the machinery and hands to pass this should not be problematic. Hulls formed from grp can be found to have spread apart at deck height and they will need to

be pulled in to the correct beam before the deck beams are fitted. Some tool catalogues list small picture cramps that extend to 12 or 15 inches and these are ideal for pulling in the sides of a hull and holding them until adhesives are cured. Alternatively you can use strong cord and a length of thin dowel in the fashion of a tourniquet to achieve the same result. It is essential to reinforce joints between beams and hull stringers with small triangles of scrap timber, particularly where hulls have been drawn in to correct width. Always allow adequate drying time for adhesives before removing clamps or tourniquets.

Having fitted the deck beams, 1.5mm thick plywood was cut to fit over the beams and form the main decks of the model. This was easily done by holding the ply firmly to the hull and drawing a sharp pencil round the perimeter to outline the shape. Note that on this model the bulwarks were to be fitted later using a finer plywood than that of the hull planking. Most grp hulls are moulded with the bulwarks already built in thus the deck supports need to be fitted at the correct level and the decks cut to fit inside the hull. With Academus it was an easy matter to cut the decks, glue and pin them in place using PVA adhesive and then to trim them accurately to the sides of the hull once the glue had cured. Small brass pins used to hold the plywood decks in place were easily sanded flush to the ply and concealed under subsequent work or painting.

Time was allowed for the work to dry out thoroughly before proceeding further. At the bow the blocks forming the shape of the model were left projecting high above the main deck as they would form the basis of the forward shelter later. Bulwarks of 0.8mm ply were next made by reference to the drawings and by holding each sheet of ply in turn to the side of the hull so that the lower edge could be cut to conform to the sheer of the main deck. Each bulwark was then carefully measured at 30mm intervals so that the increasing curves from stern towards the bow could be drawn in and the ply cut. Fitting the bulwarks was done by first gluing a 1.5mm thick x 2.0mm wide strip of timber to the main decks and setting this at 0.8mm from the outside edge of the deck to form a landing for the bulwark ply. Using cyanoacrylate (superglue) the bulwarks were fitted and left to set; although superglue provides an almost instant grab it is necessary to allow some hours to elapse before working on such joints. The bulwarks were thus glued in place as the last task one evening and the model left until next day before carrying out further work. To complete this section of the work bulwark supports cut from 1.5mm styrene were made and fitted at intervals to stiffen and hold the bulwarks in place as in the full-size vessel. Capping rails were cut from 0.8mm plywood and glued to the top of the bulwarks and the supports using superglue, small gaps being filled with fine filler once the glue had set. Finally, the blocks forming the bow were sanded to correct shape, a shelter-deck top cut from 1.5mm ply was made and glued in place and trimmed to suit the shape of the bow.

Sanding and finishing the bulwarks and bow to match the rest of the hull was next done and the whole hull was given three coats of grey primer - the type of primer filler available from auto accessory shops such as Halfords imparts a good smooth finish to timber which, after sanding lightly with fine wet-and-dry abrasive paper, can simulate steel.

After allowing adequate drying time the hull was carefully inspected for blemishes and slight imperfections were sanded or filled before pro-

ceeding. The entire hull was sprayed with acrylic red oxide (Halfords) from spray cans, three coats being applied once more, each coat being examined and sanded lightly before the next was applied.

Further drying time was allowed before the lower hull was masked off to the waterline and the upper hull given three coats of matt black acrylic. At this time too, a suitable cradle to hold the model was constructed of medium density fibre-board (MDF) and padded on the upper curved surfaces to protect the paintwork from damage. Once the black paint had been allowed to dry out thoroughly the masking was removed and the hull was examined; there were no obvious faults and to give further protection the hull was given two coats of matt varnish by spray and set aside to dry. No details of the hull lining, ship's name, port of registry or depth markings were available so this would have to wait until the full-size ship neared completion before the correct details could be applied.

Chapter 12   Inshore and middle distant fishing boats

The influence of the combustion engine upon the fishing vessel was profound and long lasting. Apart from preserved and museum-owned ships there are no steam-driven fishing boats to be found today. No naval architect would dream of designing a steam-driven fishing boat - economy and capital cost would not permit it. The modern compression ignition engine, whether it is using diesel oil (gas oil) or the heavier grades is a highly efficient prime mover and one of considerable longevity and reliability. There are few fishing vessels where one sees any sign of neglect in the engine-room or engine spaces. Kept clean and regularly serviced, the oil engine will run for very long periods with complete reliability and economy. There have been many developments recently in the types of propellers and drives that are attached to the engine, all designed to reduce the running costs and to make the ship more efficient.

The inshore fishing vessels and those that work only in the middle distant waters are, almost without exception, driven by conventional screw propellers. Often these are fitted into Kort nozzles to improve efficiency and some of these ships are fitted with bulbous bows which, despite appearances, also improve the sea-keeping qualities of the ship. Some of the larger fishing boats can be found to have variable pitch screw propellers with the engine running at constant speed for maximum economy and where the position of the propeller blades can be controlled electro-hydraulically from the bridge to move the ship ahead or astern and at almost infinitely variable speed in both directions. Today too, the modern fishing craft is controlled almost entirely from the bridge - speed, direction, winch control, net haulage etc. is all remotely controlled from bridge consoles. Modern instrumentation advises the master even of the quantity of the fish in the net so that he can decide when to haul in the catch. Fish finding, satellite navigation, ship-to-shore telephony and computer-controlled equipment require the modern skipper to acquire knowledge far in excess of the skippers of yesterday who sailed and caught their fish by the 'seat of their pants'. In the 1930s, during the depression years, over a thousand herring drifters followed the shoals through the North Sea crowding the ports as they went with catches of many thousands of tons of fish. This is now a thing of the past; modern fishing is restricted to ensure that fish stocks remain at sensible levels. Net mesh sizes are designed to allow the small young fish to escape and to mature before they can be caught.

The modern inshore and middle distant fishing vessels fish with much more modern equipment, sophisticated winches, well, carefully designed and controlled nets, all under the watchful eyes of the fishery patrols of the host countries and to the rules laid down by the European community. In a similar manner fishing is being controlled in other parts of the world and, while there are now very many fewer fishing boats to be found round our shores, the fishermen do have much better conditions and can make a reasonable living.

The inshore fishing boats of today are specifically designed to catch particular species of fish. For example, the *Academus* is designed for scallop dredging in the waters near to the Solway Firth on the west coast of Scotland and is therefore fitted with a suitable winch and an engine of adequate power for such work. The outfit of goalpost mast, foremast and derricks are all geared to the methods used for bringing the scallops to the nets. Other vessels recently seen, and of which I have built scale models, include seine net boats designed to catch those fish that swim and feed near the surface using purse seine nets sized and designed for such work.

The seine net or fly dragging is used to catch bottom fish whereas the purse seine is for catching pelagic fish and the sketches here indicate how they are spread and used. As stated earlier, many

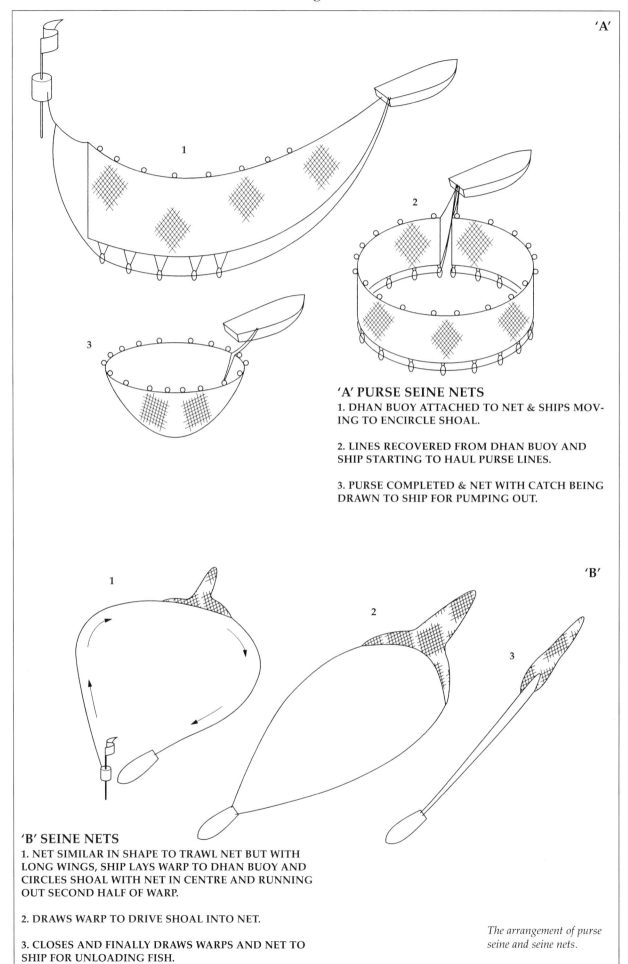

'A'

'A' PURSE SEINE NETS
1. DHAN BUOY ATTACHED TO NET & SHIPS MOVING TO ENCIRCLE SHOAL.

2. LINES RECOVERED FROM DHAN BUOY AND SHIP STARTING TO HAUL PURSE LINES.

3. PURSE COMPLETED & NET WITH CATCH BEING DRAWN TO SHIP FOR PUMPING OUT.

'B'

'B' SEINE NETS
1. NET SIMILAR IN SHAPE TO TRAWL NET BUT WITH LONG WINGS, SHIP LAYS WARP TO DHAN BUOY AND CIRCLES SHOAL WITH NET IN CENTRE AND RUNNING OUT SECOND HALF OF WARP.

2. DRAWS WARP TO DRIVE SHOAL INTO NET.

3. CLOSES AND FINALLY DRAWS WARPS AND NET TO SHIP FOR UNLOADING FISH.

The arrangement of purse seine and seine nets.

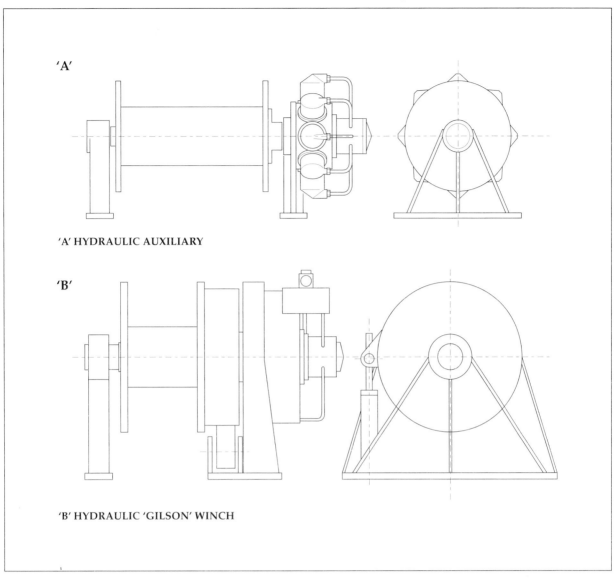

'A'

'A' HYDRAULIC AUXILIARY

'B'

'B' HYDRAULIC 'GILSON' WINCH

Drawings of typical hydraulic winches.

The purse seiner model Denebula *under construction and showing the three-quarter length shelter deck before the deck machinery is fitted.*

seiners pump the fish from the nets into the fish-room but on the smaller boats, manual handling with winch haulage is still in use. Some of these types of ship sail out to the middle distant waters

and their voyages will last seven to ten days, while those ships sailing inshore will generally sail daily and usually in the evening in order to catch the fish when they rise to feed in the early hours of the morning. Modern electronic equipment and sonar-type instruments can tell the ship's master when shoals of fish are close and from this data he can position his ship and the nets to maximum advantage. It is no lie to say that the modern fishing vessel can catch more fish in a single voyage that the early vessels caught in four.

In addition to those boats which sail to catch swimming fish there are those that are designed and sail to catch the crabs and lobsters and other types of shellfish. Crabs and lobsters are generally caught in pots baited and placed on the sea bed. Lobster and crab pots are, in effect, open-work baskets with an entrance designed to allow the crab or lobster to enter and feed but not to escape once inside. The location of the pots is

The hydraulic anchor windlass on the stern trawler Glenrose 1. *Note the black and white marked rod used to permit measuring from the photograph.*

usually indicated by small buoys attached to the line of pots and with a flag on the rod fixed to the buoy. The crabber boat, generally quite small, will generally attend to the pots on a daily basis, bringing in the catch to market early and fresh for good prices. Such small craft are usually in the hands of but two (quite frequently) members of the same family, perhaps father and son or brothers. The return can be small and seasonal but there is usually a good demand for quality shellfish.

Using well designed, compact and seaworthy craft will be found the fisherman who trawls the inshore and middle distant waters for those fish the swim near the ocean bed. Among such fish will be found the cod and haddock beloved by the fried fish shops in the UK but they will also catch plaice, halibut and similar flat fish. These ships are often built to be multi-purpose to work according to season and area; they will on some voyages, load trawl nets and otter boards and go trawling for deep-swimming fish and for other trips, load nets and equipment to catch the pelagic fish. The range of winches available to the ship owner and shipbuilder of today is vast and the outfit of winches needed for efficient fish net handling can be costly.

A side view of the model of the stern trawler Glenrose 1.

The smaller ships will be more likely to have their auxiliaries run by electric power from the alternator fitted to the main engine and usually driven from the main shaft through a power take-off. The larger ships of today usually use winches driven hydraulically with the hydraulic pumps, either driven from the main engine shaft or separately driven by electric motors, with the pumps housed below decks in a purpose-built pump-room or space in the engine-room. The hydraulically driven deck auxiliaries are much less prone to problems in the damp atmosphere of the working decks of a fishing boat and less

Gilson pattern hydraulic winch on the stern trawler Glenrose 1.

Cod-end winch also using hydraulic drive on Glenrose 1.

liable to problems of freezing in arctic winter conditions. Such hydraulic auxiliaries can be controlled readily from the bridge using electropneumatic controls but they are also easily controlled locally when necessary. Some illustrations of such machinery are shown and there are some sketches to provide the would-be modeller with some data.

For those who wish to build good model fishing vessels it is well to carry out sensible research into all aspects of the chosen ship subject. Skippers, particularly skipper/owners, that frequent the small fishing ports round the coasts of the UK are generally very proud of their ships and happy to show them to the interested modeller. In general, a polite request to permit the taking of photographs, particularly once a catch has been landed and disposed of ashore, will often result in an invitation to go on board, and such a visit can provide a wealth of valuable information when building the model. One never seems to take enough photographs when visiting a ship and the one needed to sort out that particular hatchway or fitting is always the one that has been missed. When visiting a given ship I try to find out, in advance, whether there will be the chance of a second visit and if not, then I take at least six rolls of film to cover the ship from stem to stern.

In the case of *Glenrose* illustrated here, some four visits were made to the ship and well over 100 hundred pictures were taken. In the case of *Academus* the shipyard was visited a total of 10 times during the time it was being built and, once more, some 80 to 90 photographs were obtained, all to ensure accuracy. Obviously it is not possible for every modeller to visit the ship he/she has

The net winch on Glenrose 1.

chosen to build, especially if it no longer sails in home waters or has, perhaps, been broken up or been wrecked. For this reason as many illustrations of deck fittings and details as possible are included here to aid the builder.

Regretfully too, the demise of the shipbuilding industry in the UK makes visits to working yards out of the question and most modellers have thus to rely upon the experiences of others who have either worked in the industry or were involved in shipping business. Such second-hand information, as long as it is accurate, is the only means one has of gaining the necessary knowledge into the fasci-

The wheelhouse on Academus *with windows masked and surfaces prepared for painting white.*

nating world of the ship. The good modeller will store such data carefully against future needs and pass on assistance, particularly to the young and blossoming modeller, so that the craft of ship modelling will carry on. I have seen some amusing things over the years, for example, spending a camping holiday in the Galloway area of Scotland there were a number of keen fishermen who sailed in the bay each evening to try for mackerel. They had little success, but three small boys, no more than ten or twelve years of age had a dinghy out nearby, and using lines with white feathers as lures they hauled in fish after fish, much to the chagrin of the men. To make things worse, the boys proceeded to sell their mackerel to the fishermen's wives back at the campsite. I can vouch for the full flavour of those freshly caught blue and silver beauties.

Academus - Foredeck and superstructure

The next stage in the construction of *Academus* was the completion of the forecastle deck and the building of the main superstructure. The foredeck having been cut and fitted was next fitted with curtain plates cut from 0.8mm thick plywood. Curtain plates are those pieces of plate which are cut and fitted to the edges of overhanging deck in much the same way as a pelmet is fitted over a window or door. In general the curtain plating projects slightly above the edge of the deck or the deck timbers to form a slight ledge and projects downward anywhere from 150mm to 200mm. In the case of *Academus* the curtain plates were some 200mm deep. There is one distinct advantage in fitting and gluing curtain plates carefully to the edges of exposed decks in that they strengthen the edges and render the overhanging deck sections much stronger than they would otherwise be. Careful examination of full-size ships will show that overhanging decks are also supported at regular intervals by beams of steel plate welded in place and usually at the same intervals as the main frames of the ship - such intervals are, today, generally at 600mm centres. The plywood curtain plates were glued in place with cyanoacrylate of the thick type to gain a quick grab and to also have a degree of gap filling. At least 24 hours were allowed to elapse before any attempt was made to sand and dress these plates and to give them the needed coats of white acrylic paint.

There were difficulties experienced in the building of *Academus* due mainly to the yard making alterations during construction at the request of the owner. This affected the accuracy of the drawings provided and required frequent site visits to verify each stage of model building. For example, the main superstructure was found to be slightly inac-

curate when the model was examined just before it was handed over and at a time much too late to effect any alteration. The length of the port side aft from stern to the break, just behind the location of the large beam and block, was found to be some 500mm longer than on the starboard side but the model showed both sides of equal length. Thankfully this is not too obvious and can only be seen by careful examination of both the model and the full-size vessel at the same time.

The superstructure was built entirely from white styrene sheet using three differing thicknesses (2.0mm, 1.5mm and 1.0mm) to allow strength and yet provide fine detail. Of fairly simple box shape and built in a series of interlinking boxes it became particularly rigid and strong as the work proceeded. Styrene sheet joined using liquid polystyrene cement is quick and clean in use - the surface requires virtually no preparation before being painted although the choice of paint needs to be made with care. Paint with a cellulose base will attack the sheet and mar the surface but modern car enamels and the acrylic paints in use today are safe. The model enamels such as Humbrol and Precision paints will adhere well to the styrene but it is always wise to prime the surfaces with a good undercoating primer before applying finish colours.

Each piece of the superstructure was measured and cut to fit in place on the deck of the model, the locations of windows and portlights were marked off and cut out before any attempt was made at assembly. When cutting styrene sheet use a sharp craft knife and a steel rule, preferably with the work being done on a self-healing cutting mat. You will find that the edge of the cut sheet develops a slight lip. This lip should be gently sanded or scraped away with the knife blade on edge before joining the parts together - it is much easier then than after assembly. To effect a good joint hold the parts together firmly and apply the liquid polystyrene cement to the top of the joint using a small brush. The liquid will be drawn into the joint by capillary action and the joint will be welded quite firmly within a few seconds. Do not assume that this fast welding is fully secure however and wait at least 4 to 5 hours before attempting to sand or dress the joint to allow the solvents to evaporate properly. Some people will find the smell unpleasant while others can be affected by the solvents reacting upon sinuses etc. For safety always work in a well-ventilated atmosphere and, if in doubt, wear a face mask - it is better to be safe than sorry. I suffer from asthma and find that while the cyanoacrylate glues do affect breathing, with the workshop well vented it is not too serious a problem. You are, of course, using only very small quantities and bottles and cans should always be kept closed firmly when the liquid is not needed. Liquid polystyrene evaporates very quickly and it takes but a short time for a large bottle to disappear if the top is left open.

Building a simple structure such as was needed for Academus is not difficult but thought is still needed. When tackling such jobs, ensure that those spaces which will become inaccessible as the work proceeds are not going to be visible through windows or portholes and, if they are, then consider applying paint or fitting in furniture before they are closed up. In those places where you need to run wires and cables for lights or hoses to feed fire monitors etc., ensure that provision is made, either for access or that the necessary parts are fitted as the superstructure is built. Recently, when building a model of a small bunkering tanker, the fitting of the two anchor boxes at the bow were omitted and went unnoticed until the hull was painted and the decks had been fitted. Making and retro-fitting these two boxes was anything but easy with access severely restricted, to say nothing of the possible damage to the paintwork which was happily avoided. Always try to see at least two steps ahead and pre-plan the work to avoid such snags - we are all human and even the best of us do make mistakes.

The wheelhouse or, perhaps one should say the bridge, is an area which merits care and attention to detail. The modern ship rarely has a wheel as most steering is done by means of a joystick very similar to those used with computer games, and much of the ship's guidance is done automatically with an autopilot and satellite navigation controls. This house, however, is given large windows frequently shaped to shed water easily and to provide first-class visibility so the interior is very easily viewed on a model of reasonable size. With luck some of the drawings will give some detail of the bridge interior and allow you to simulate the control desk, monitor screens etc. and also to make and fit a suitable seat for the master or helmsman. Much of the bridge interior today is carried out using formica or similar plastic-faced timber, often with simulated wood graining, as this material is easy to keep clean and very resistant to the elements. Thus, where no photographs can be obtained or data gained, it will not be too

difficult to give your model bridge at least a look of the real thing.

One of the problems that faces the marine modeller is the fitting of glazing material to the windows of the model. Many transparent sheets are seriously marred by modern glues such as super-glue and liquid polystyrene cement and sometimes this fault does not show up until days after the glazing has been fastened in. Superglue can make some glazing go milky after a few days. Look for transparent styrene sheet - note 'styrene' sheet (not just plastic sheet) - as this can be safely glued to white styrene using liquid polystyrene cement. Otherwise glazing is best secured using thin strips of double-sided adhesive tape or with the glazing slotted into channels formed round the window openings. Remember always to paint the superstructure before fixing the glazing and obviously provide for fitting the roof or the floor after such access has been used to paint the interior and fit the glazing.

On particularly large scale models it is possible to make and fit individual panes of glazing where there are surrounds to fit both outside and inside the window apertures, and in this case no adhesive is necessary. Where glazing is needed for portlights (portholes) located close to the waterline and where water can penetrate easily it is very necessary to ensure that such glazing is secure. In such cases I invariably use slow-curing epoxy glue to fix the glazing; slow cure because it is the only type of epoxy glue that is not affected by water once it has cured and also because it will easily fill small gaps and keep the joints proof against water entering.

The photographs and sketches illustrate the superstructure of Academus much more easily that can be described in words. A simple task which took but a couple of days (possibly 10 hours) to draw up, cut out and assemble. Some of the edges needed to be sanded lightly to blend them to their neighbours and there were one or two small areas to which lightweight filler was applied to fill depressions. A light rub over with warm water and detergent to remove the grease of fingers during handling was all that was needed prior to applying the paint.

Chapter 13 Specialist fishing vessels

In more recent years many of the fishing communities and large fishing families have moved into specialist fish seeking and catching, using vessels built with sophisticated refrigeration equipment and designed to stay at sea for longer periods. This allows their searches for fish to be made much further from their home ports and also to sell their catches in ports where high prices can be gained. This area of development seems to be mainly in the search for pelagic fish known to feed close to the surface, and some fishing boat owners have elected to have very large ships built for this type of service. Most of these large pelagic fishing boats seem to be built on the European mainland in Denmark, Holland and frequently in Norway or Finland. Most are up to and over 70 metres long and can accommodate crews of 10 to 15. All have highly developed fish searching electronic instrumentation; the facility to clean and gut catches and to provide suitable refrigeration plant to keep the catch in good order for voyages having a duration in excess of eight weeks.

Almost all are suitable for seine and purse seine netting with a back-up of trawling facilities and some extremely complex and cleverly designed equipment is used to great advantage. These ships travel long distances to find fish, often travelling from the UK to the waters around Newfoundland and in the North Atlantic. These trips can, particularly in winter, be very hazardous. The days of cleaning and gutting fish on the open decks and in the face of high seas have, of course, long gone. Modern fishing vessels have fish treatment rooms below deck where, in hygenic conditions working with stainless steel equipment in stainless lined areas, the fish are treated and passed to the storage areas. There is little chance of the model shipbuilder producing a working scale model which actually includes a fish processing room made in stainless steel, but the fact that such facilities are in place on the ship means that the deck layout is much different. On the old steam- and motor-driven trawlers and many of the herring drifters, sec-tions of the forward decks were fitted with 9 or 12 inch high partitions of timber planks slotted into angle guides to form ponds in which the cleaned fish were sorted prior to be boxed and stowed below. With bulwarks in these areas little more than 0.66 metres high, fish ponds were constantly being swept with water in high seas and, as previously mentioned, it was not unknown for men to be washed overboard with little chance of being saved.

Modern fishing methods which are largely controlled from the bridge of the ship mean that seamen and fishermen spend much less time on the open decks, furthermore the working parts of the decks carry very high bulwarks today making the work much less hazardous - that is not to say that the work is less arduous but good winches and draw gear does help. The *Glenrose* illustrated is a typical example of a trawler built within the last few years and it will be noticed that the bulwarks on either side of the main deck are just over 3 metres high. To allow access to this deck when the ship is in port there are doors in the plating just aft of the accommodation on both sides of the ship and these doors are sealed shut once the ship is underway.

Regretfully at the time of writing, I was unable to obtain drawings of the large new pelagic fishing vessels within the time constraints of going to press. Within newspapers such as Fishing News and some of the magazines published for the fishing fraternity can be found illustrations of these very large vessels. Some can now be found within the Scottish Owners register and many more hail from Ireland - all huge by present-day standards. All appear to have a single oil engine, invariably driving a variable pitch propeller within a Kort-type nozzle, and all also seem to sport at least one bow thruster set athwartships. Some have both bow and stern thrusters, and one has been seen to have two bow and one stern thruster. Easy movement in the confined areas of small fishing ports

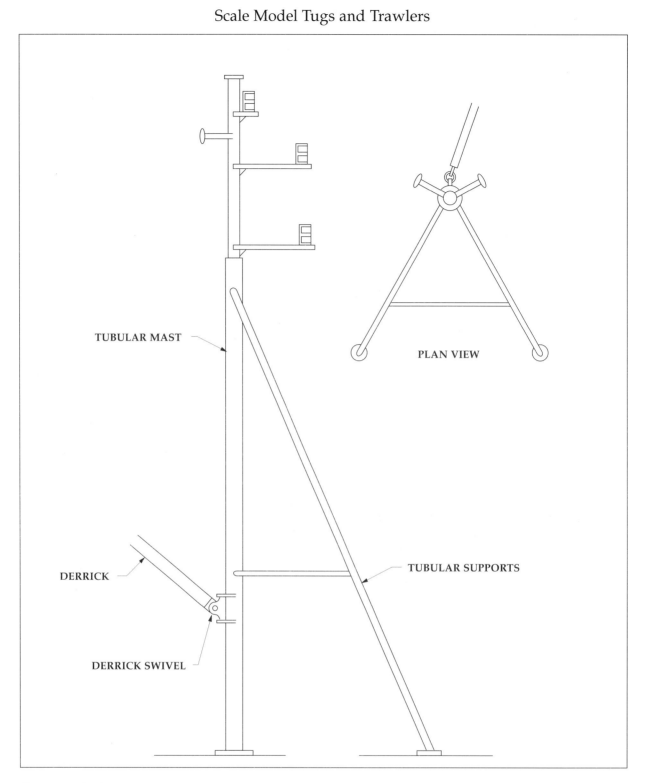

TUBULAR MAST

PLAN VIEW

DERRICK

TUBULAR SUPPORTS

DERRICK SWIVEL

Foremast on Academus.

where, quite often prices for fish can be very good, is obviously a matter of priority.

There is little doubt that drawings of such ships will soon be made available to the modeller although naval architects do tend to keep their development secrets well hidden for some time. These large ships carry a wealth of winches to carry out the work of shooting and hauling the nets, regardless of the purpose for which the nets are needed.

To assist the marine modeller seeking to build a good and accurate fishing boat there are included a number of drawings and sizing charts depicting winches of various sizes, duties and operations. Most makers of such equipment are generally happy to assist a keen modeller provided that requests are made politely, in legible writing and preferably accompanied by a stamped and self-addressed envelope for a reply. Catalogues of their wares can often be found at some of the large trade exhibitions held annually in many parts of

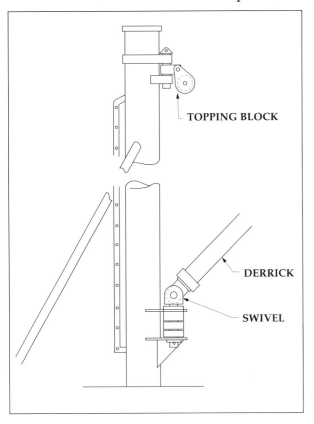

Derrick and swivel for Academus.

model ship - many hours need to be spent in research and many more making visits, if possible, to the actual ship to take photographs and measurements of all the deck machinery and fittings. Building the model from a kit avoids much of this effort but does, sometimes, spoil the fun and excitement of spending time on a real vessel. Despite the many books and magazines available today dealing with all aspects of ships, where possible, even if the model is being constructed from a kit, the builder should endeavour to see the real thing 'in the flesh' so to speak. In this way you can absorb the atmosphere of the ship and, to some degree, repeat it in the model. Bearing in mind the number of trades that are involved in the building of the ship it behoves you to at least seek to examine some of the real work closely so that you can reproduce it with care. The joy of completing a working model and seeing it sail for the very first time is something to be treasured, and the joy of visiting a real ship and showing the crew the model of it built with care and attention is even greater. When the model of *Academus* was presented to her new owner at the naming and handing-over ceremony of the full-size ship, it brought tears to his eyes with pleasure and there are no coins in any currency that can pay that well for a model. The watchword is build with care and enjoy.

Academus - winch, masts and rigging

Returning to *Academus* the deckhouse, having been completed and painted, was set aside while funnel, foremast, goalposts and main mast were

the country and these give a great deal of detail. Best of all is the contact made with the owners or, perhaps, the shipbuilder where the exact size of winch in each location will be known precisely.

It is impossible for any writer to provide all the information that is needed to build an accurate

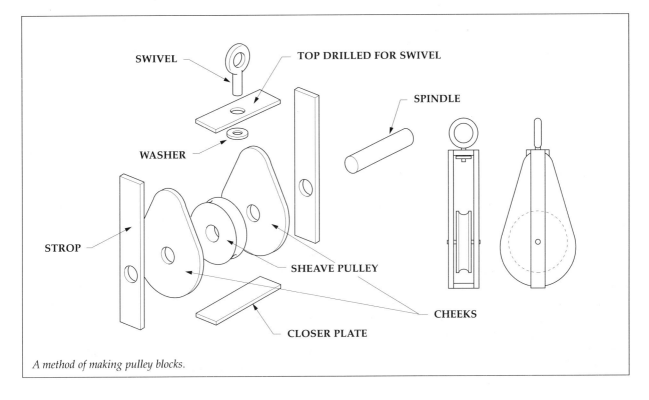

A method of making pulley blocks.

built and the North Sea Winches unit was replicated in timber with wire and styrene fittings. The winch was tackled first. Suitable timber (a block of applewood) was shaped and fitted into a drill/lathe and turned to give the whole length of the drums, rope guides etc. This was finished with very fine sandpaper and sealed with sanding sealer. The carrier frames and ends were fashioned from timber and styrene scrap and the shafts for the control wheels were made from brass wire. The actual handwheels were of etched nickel silver from James Lane (Display Models) and were secured to the shafts with superglue. Most of the winch was glued together using white PVA adhesive and, after allowing adequate time for the glue and sealer to dry out the whole unit was sprayed with bright blue acrylic paint to match the full-size unit. Once dry it was mounted on runners made from styrene channel sections and then fitted to the model.

Masts can be problematic and decisions must be made regarding the material from which to make them and how it will be fashioned. Such decisions are governed by the use to which the model will be put and whether or not functioning lighting will be installed. In the case of *Academus* there was little to be concerned over - the ship model was to be fitted into a glass display case, there were to be no operating lights and the model was never likely to be subject to the rigours of regatta sailing on the local lake. Styrene tube from the Plastruct and Evergreen ranges would adequately serve the purpose for this model.

Foremast

The foremast is of simple tripod construction, the main mast being of parallel tubes in two sizes as shown in the sketch here. There are two supports of smaller size tube arranged to brace the main section in a tripod style and these are interconnected by horizontal bracing tubes approximately halfway up the sloping braces. The top of the mast, made of more slender tube, carries the navigation lamps and is capped with a small flat plate. Running up the forward face of the mast is a steel ladder to give access to the running lights and a substantial derrick is swivel-mounted from the back of the mast near the base. Details of the derrick, its swivel and the rigging attached to it, are shown in the accompanying sketches and pictures.

If you require this mast to be fitted with functioning lights, then the sensible course would be to make the mast of brass tube. Suitable brass tubing can be bought from most model shops, sized so that the smaller bore tubes are a neat sliding fit in

A model of Glenrose 1. *Note the high bulwarks forward of the gantry and up to the boat deck.*

The winch on the scallop dredger Academus. *Note the large size - this winch is over 2 metres across full size.*

the next larger size. Assembling a brass tube mast is fairly easy using soft solder and a good iron in place of the liquid polystyrene cement used for the plastic unit. The main advantage of the metal mast is in its strength to withstand small knocks and the fact that the metal can act as the return or negative when cabling up to the navigation lamps. This cuts down the number of wires that need to be led through the tubes and avoids too many joints which have to be insulated and still fitted into the tube of the mast.

Once the mast of *Academus* was assembled it was painted white and fitted into a correctly drilled locating hole in the fore or shelter deck. Great care is needed when fitting the masting and rigging to any ship model. It is all too easy to pull a mast out of truth with the rigging cord if the mast is not sighted carefully from both sides and from ahead and astern to ensure correct lining up. There is, of course, no standing rigging fitted to the foremast of *Academus* but many ships do have standing rigging.

Standing rigging is the terminology applied to all wire and hempen ropes used on board a ship to support a mast or structure. This rigging 'stands' as tensioned, it is not used for any other purpose than supports. Standing rigging is almost invariably steel wire rope on the ship of today and such rigging is almost always set up using rigging screws or 'bottle screws' to apply tension. It is possible to purchase working rigging screws in a number of sizes from those model shops specialising in model ships.

Running rigging is all that ropework that runs through blocks and pulleys (sheaves) and that is used for handling cargo, moving stores, hauling weights of all kinds - even down to controlling a 'bosun's chair' to lift the master on board from a boat when the ship is high in the water and the gangway is not long enough to reach. There are a great many differing types of rope block used for the many jobs on board a ship. Those found on the small fishing vessel are, thankfully, few and some are shown in the sketches together with the method used to rope them up. Although lifeboats are rarely seen on fishing boats today, their blocks and rigging are a feature to be found on many larger vessels and bear examination if the opportunity presents. Most fishing boats of today carry a rigid inflatable boat slung under a small crane or derrick for everyday use, and also a number of liferafts encased in canisters (taking up little space) for quick release and inflation in an emergency. Such safety devices must be tested at regular intervals as part of the vessel's surveys and all members of the crew must be fully educated with regard to their use.

On *Academus* my photographs found only one canister which would be quite adequate for a crew of only three or four persons. This canister was mounted in a small cradle on the top of the aft section of the superstructure where it could be easily reached and pitched overboard when necessary. This small ship is unlikely ever to sail in the deep and dangerous waters of the northern oceans, so that the provisions for life-saving, which include life-jackets for every crew member, are perfectly acceptable to the ruling survey bodies. It is a sad fact that very few people can survive the shock of instant immersion in sea water which has temperatures below freezing - they do

The foremast on Academus.

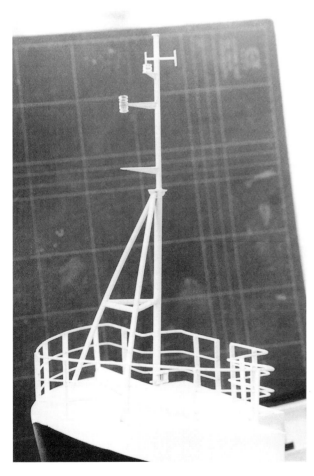

The foremast under construction for Academus.

not drown but literally freeze to death in seconds - and there is very rarely enough time to turn a ship round and find the person who has been swept overboard before they succumb. The sea is a treacherous place in which to seek a living by fishing with nets and the men who make this their life's work are to be admired.

Goalpost masts

Moving aft on *Academus* we come to the 'goalpost' so named because it resembles a rugby football set of goalposts. This mast system carries two derricks, one to port and the other to starboard, used to bring the nets inboard and for unloading the catch. On top of the crossbar are fitted a radar unit and four radio aerials. There is an access ladder to reach the radio equipment and other parts. This mast is very substantially built of steel tube on the full-size ship; the base is bolted securely to the main deck and it is braced from the front of the bridge unit with short tubes while longer tubes support it at high level off the bridge top. In the same way as the foremast was constructed, styrene tube of various sizes was used and firmly cemented together using liquid polystyrene cement. It is necessary to shape the ends of the tubes to match the location in which they fit before applying the cement and it is always necessary to allow at least twelve hours for the cement to cure before proceeding too far. The sketches and pictures show the general construction of this unit and there is a copy of the shipbuilder's detail drawing to aid potential modellers. As previously mentioned it would be possible to make a much more substantial unit using brass tube although the end result would look much the same. The styrene goalpost had working derricks although they were not really necessary - they were made just to verify that operational derricks could be done in this material.

Main mast and funnel

Finally the funnel unit and main mast were made from styrene sheet and tube to match the photographs and drawing of the real ship as closely as possible. Of a fairly complex shape it took just a couple of days to build up but some degree of pre-planning was necessary to obtain the correct shape. A couple of abortive attempts were made before the funnel was deemed to be correct. We all make mistakes and there is no need to be ashamed of it so long as we learn by them and put things right in the end - shocking waste of time though. Once more there are photographs to show the construction which is easier to see than to describe.

All the masting, derricks etc. were painted white before being installed on the ship. The most time-

The main mast of Academus *mounted on top of the wheelhouse.*

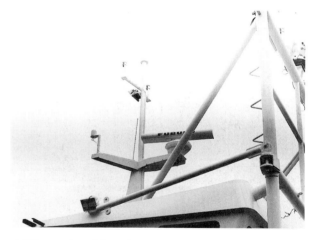

A different view of the main mast on Academus *showing part of the goalpost.*

consuming task in regard to this work was, without doubt, the making of the rope blocks. As far as can be ascertained no blocks of modern outline seem to be available from commercial manufacturers, thus the three different sizes each had to be made from scratch. Some were single sheave, some were double sheave and two were triple sheave pattern. All were made in the same way as shown in the accompanying sketch and all took time to get right. The sheaves (pulleys) were cut and grooved from plastic knitting needles of suitable diameter. Such knitting needles are a valu-

Part of the goalpost assembly on Academus.

A general view of the masts and goalpost on Academus.

The model goalpost under construction.

able source of accurate round rod. Where they carry a label stating 8mm they are exactly 8mm diameter and 6mm is exactly 6mm etc. The smaller needles are, regretfully, usually made of aluminium and thus not so useful but the plastic ones go as high as 15mm in solid form with some larger sizes formed from tubular stock - a visit to the local haberdashery shop may result in a stock of rods at a reasonable cost (they make fine bollards too).

Handrails

Moving on to the upper decks next led to the making and fixing of the handrails round the main superstructure and the shelter deck, and initially consideration was given to making the handrail stanchions from brass with the rails also in brass but of two sizes. The time needed to set up a jig for cutting and boring the brass sheet and how to mount the brass rails was carefully considered and finally rejected in favour of making the rails in styrene. A small jig was made in which the stanchions could be drilled accurately after they were cut from 1.0mm sheet and this was attached to the pedestal drill. The top bar of the rails is almost twice the diameter of the two lower bars.

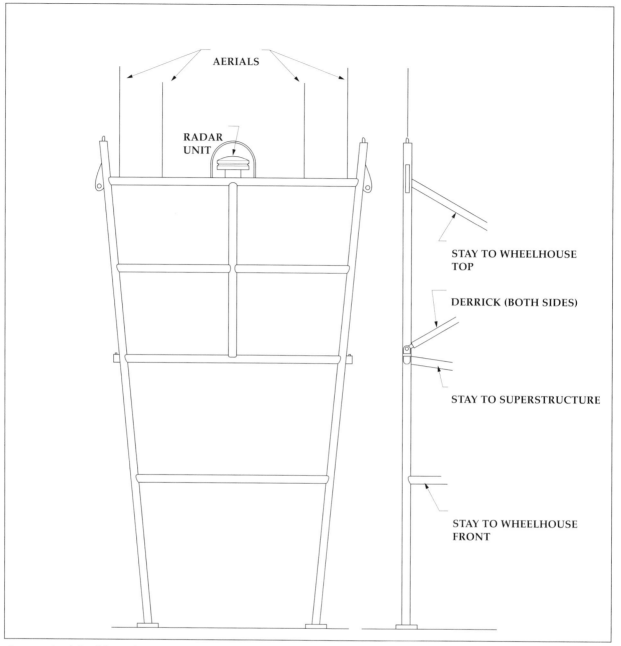

AERIALS

RADAR
UNIT

STAY TO WHEELHOUSE
TOP

DERRICK (BOTH SIDES)

STAY TO SUPERSTRUCTURE

STAY TO WHEELHOUSE
FRONT

Constructional detail for goalpost mast to suit a small scallop dredger

On the real ship the top bar is welded to the top of the steel stanchions while the lower bars are threaded through suitably bored holes before being welded. The styrene stanchions and rails were made in much the same way, the top bar being formed from 1.5mm plastic-coated wire was welded to the stanchions using superglue whereas the lower bars of 1.0mm dia styrene rod were threaded through the stanchion holes and tacked in place with liquid polystyrene cement. The rails were made off the model and assembled over drawings on balsa into which the stanchions were pressed at the precise intervals. Once the glue had been allowed time to cure properly, the assembled rails were painted with white acrylic from a spray and set aside to dry before being fixed to the model into holes bored in the deckhead where required and secured with liquid polystyrene cement. This method of assembling ship's rails is perfectly suited to a large model for display purposes but would not necessarily be suitable for a model that is to be sailed and operated where a more substantial rail is needed. A number of kit manufacturers have brass and/or nickel silver stanchions of the flat bar pattern in etched form that may be suitable for a scale model of large size.

Chapter 14   Service vessels and research

There are a number of (ancillary) ships that may be said to be attached to the fishing industry. First there is the bunkering tanker, which supplies the fuel oil and similar liquids needed by the fishing boats. A typical example of a bunkering tanker is illustrated. Small and highly specialised, it is designed and built exactly for the purpose of refuelling ships of all sizes. A bunkering tanker makes a fine and unusual model and the one illustrated will be marketed in kit form during 1999 by Deans Marine and is based upon my research and design work. Bunkering tankers can be found in almost all the large ports throughout the world, generally tied to a larger vessel and busy loading fuel. The very large rubber fenders are distinctive and are seen mostly on this type of vessel.

The *Rix Harrier* illustrated is driven by twin azimuth thrusters from two Caterpillar oil engines; the drive system incorporates gears giving an effective reduction between engine and screw of 4:1 thus reducing engine speed from approximately 1000 rpm to 250 rpm at the propeller. The azimuth thruster with the ability to turn through 360 degrees gives the ship superb turning ability so that positioning alongside other vessels can be very precise. It should be noted, however, that this type of ship has very low freeboard - the main deck on *Rix Harrier* is only 0.6 metres above the water when she is fully laden. On a scale model at 1:50 this means a water to main deck level of just 15 millimetres (just over 0.5 inches).

Sealing the deck to the coaming of the main hatch or tank cover needs to be well done to avoid ingress of water when sailing on anything other than flat calm water. This type of ship would make a fine model, however, and it would be well worthwhile looking out for one during port or harbour visits.

Each year, off the coast of Scotland and sometimes in the Scottish ports, there will be found a

The bunkering tanker Rix Harrier *pictured in Alexandra Dock, Hull.*

A nicely detailed model of a steam launch at the lakeside during a sailing regatta.

number of 'Klondykers', ships which come from the Russian and Eastern Baltic ports to buy the catches of the fishing boats even before the catches are landed. These ships are very often old trawlers or steam-driven fishing boats of large size. It is an unfortunate fact that most of them are in an appallingly poor condition, each season some are impounded until their condition is improved before they are allowed to continue. They buy all manner of fish in almost any condition to carry back to fish-processing factories for the making of fertiliser etc. There is little chance of obtaining drawings of such ships or of getting close enough to take detailed photographs however you may find some photographs in Ships

Monthly and Sea Breezes periodically. These will show you how such ships can be neglected and, of course, illustrate clearly the effect weather can have upon paintwork if it is left for long periods without attention.

Some years ago it was possible to see two large whale factory ships berthed in the River Tyne at North Shields. They sailed the southern oceans each year, their catcher ships sought the whales, speared them with harpoons and towed them to the factory ships where they were processed for their oil and meat. This practice has long ceased in the UK and, as far as can be seen there are no drawings or kits available depicting the whale factory ship. Until recently, however, one manufacturer did produce a whaler - one of the ships attached to a factory ship that went in search of the whale. This made into a fine model and it is just possible that a few of these kits can still be found.

One of the most important ships attached to the fishing community is the fishery protection vessel. This is, of course, usually a ship from the fleet of the country concerned, for example, the Royal Navy in the UK. The Scottish Office have their own protection vessels, two of which are fast patrol boats. The very latest protection vessels serve a dual purpose: they protect the fleet from interference by other ships and they board and test the nets and fishing equipment on all ships to ensure that all comply with the latest regulations. Such regulations are much too complex for discussion here but they do apply to all fishing vessels sailing in the waters round Europe and in the Atlantic.

Depending upon the station and time, the fishery protection vessel can be a standard small warship, such as a mine countermeasures vessel or small sloop etc., seconded to protection duties and thus once you have decided to build a fishery protection ship it will be necessary to seek data from plans services etc.

In addition, there are a number of finely designed and built fishery research vessels under the control of the Ministry of Agriculture, Fisheries and Food and the Scottish Office in the UK (and in various European countries) and these ships too make attractive models. A great deal of time and research will be needed to locate suitable drawings and data from which to build a model.

Not all model shipbuilders see their hobby from the same viewpoint. Some build their ships from kits as quickly as possible with the object of getting them on the water for the pleasure of sailing. Some build more slowly, savouring the pleasures

of making a fine scale model before it is placed on the water for that sailing session, and some build purely for the pleasure of building and are not concerned with sailing the finished product at all. There are also those who build models in a highly competitive way, travelling long distances to compete against fellow modellers - generally in a friendly fashion - while others build very fine static models specifically to enter them in one of the prestigious shows such as the Model Engineer Exhibition (IMS) held in London each year. All are, of course, ship modellers and whatever their reason for modelling they represent the backbone of the model ship societies and clubs throughout the world.

I fall into the category of building mainly for the pleasure of building and, although some models are fully operational, most are static models built for specific clients. I do, however, belong to a model boat club and am an active member on its ruling committee. I enjoy sailing whenever the opportunity presents but am not really competitive. You can, therefore, see that there are many aspects of model shipbuilding of which the tug

A well-weathered fishing boat sailing the course of a regatta.

A model of the Maggie M *built from a Model Slipway kit, here showing her paces at a regatta.*

A model of the tug Smit Duitsland *passing a large model cargo ship which is anchored in the lake and used as a hazard for the regatta.*

and trawler form but a part. Regatta sailing in company with other modellers is a particularly pleasant way to spend a sunny summer afternoon, such sailing need not be too competitive and most club sails are social events where the members exchange ideas and talk of methods of model building. The newcomer to model shipbuilding is well advised to seek out their local model boat club and take part in their activities. Almost all clubs welcome new members and their existing members generally have wide experience, the fruits of which they will readily pass on.

One aspect of model shipbuilding, which the kit unfortunately seems to dull, is researching into a given vessel with the view to making a model personal to the builder. We would all like to put a model ship on the water in the knowledge that no other person has yet produced one the same so that it is unique. This is often quite possible if adequate research is carried out so that the basic stern trawler is altered just enough to make it special. For example, when travelling through the city of Hull some time ago I saw a stern trawler called *Northella* in the docks there. This ship, if my memory serves me correctly, was used when research was made into the sinking of the German battleship Bismark . It is now, obviously, back in her home port and possibly back with her owners - she was in fine condition in grey paint and carried every indication of being fully operational although for what purpose I do not know. Such a ship could form the basis of a research project resulting in a model of unique value. It is possible that a kit for a similar outline ship could be found and modified to give the required finished model and this route to modelling a prototype will save considerable time. Research will take time, there are few short cuts and you need to be patient. In the first instance you will have to consult Lloyds Register of Ships, copies of which are generally

held in the major central libraries of all reasonably sized towns. Within the volumes of this register will be found all ships in service at the time of printing. The data published is wide ranging: the ship's name is followed by all the names it may have borne previously and the dates of the changes; the current owners and their addresses are logged; the size of the ship; the type of ship; the shipbuilder and the date it was built; the gross, net and deadweight tonnages are given followed by the number; size and type of engine, propulsion etc. Careful examination of the column data explanations will reveal that a great deal more information is there for those who wish to seek further. From this data you can then move to find more information, a letter to the owners asking for help will often result in some information. Similarly letters to the shipbuilder, assuming they still exist, can produce drawings and offer help. In some cases, a letter to the master of the ship will result in information and sometimes an invitation to visit and spend time on board. Bear in mind that quite often the data that you may need will be on board the ship in question, and that cannot be obtained until the ship reaches a home port which may be in a month or two.

Information on current UK fishing vessels can be obtained either from an Olsen's Almanac, the fishermen's bible or from Fishing News, a weekly periodical which contains articles on new building. Fishing News also publish yearly a comprehensive list of fishing vessels along with photographs, giving details and a lot of information with reference to owners, agents and also detailing ships' dimensions and propulsion.

If the ship concerned is one which has had a notable and newsworthy event in its time, then quite possibly such news will be logged at the premises of the principal local newspaper. It is usually possible to view the archive copies of newspapers by pre-arrangement and, for a small fee, photocopies of the relevent passages can be obtained. Should the event be one of real importance then it is possible that the local TV station covered the happening and that they too will have details on file, perhaps even a copy of the event on video. All such research needs time and effort, not only by the researcher, but also by those to whom the queries are directed and it is only polite to thank those involved for their efforts. One source not yet mentioned is the maritime museum. Many large ports and cities support a maritime museum and here can be seen models of fine ships built locally, sections of machinery and complete engine- and boiler-rooms in some cases. There will be an archive attached to the museum and access to some of the data therein can generally be gained upon request. Possibly the best known and largest of marine museums is the National Maritime Museum at Greenwich. Here is stored possibly the largest collection of marine miscellany in the world. Access to the drawings and photographs is made by writing to the appropriate custodian in the first instance. The modern museum suffers from a lack of finance these days and often it is not possible for its staff to catalogue and list all the drawings, for example, that have been passed to them when a local ship or engine builder has closed down. This is an unfortunate fact and it may be that the data or drawings required for that special project are not available. You must then seek alternative routes but research into the history of a given vessel is quite fascinating and can be enjoyed at the same time as you build.

A great many of the docks in the UK are, today, in the hands of Associated British Ports and it is not always possible to enter such areas unless prior

consent has been given. Some areas of ports are also areas where hazardous work is being undertaken and, for this reason, visits are precluded. As with all things, it is better to ask permission than to be found trespassing. Port visits are sometimes organised by the model boat clubs or societies when a conducted tour of a facility will be arranged. If you are fortunate enough to be invited to visit a given ship, do keep to the area in which the ship is located, do not wander into other areas of the docks or port and restrict your photography to the area in which you are based. In foreign countries; particularly in the Eastern bloc, photography is frowned upon and, in some places, highly illegal thus permits are essential. There is so often so much to see on board a ship that it is difficult to decide what to photograph. It is best to take shots of all the deck machinery and fittings that you will need information about when building the model. To aid such photography a stick or rod about three feet long marked in bands of black and white at 100mm intervals is a very good guide to the size of an object if it is placed close to the fitting when it is photographed. The finished print can be measured back in the workshop and the size of the fitting determined quite accurately from the marked divisions on the rod or stick.

Academus - deck planking, fittings and finish

Returning to *Academus* deck details were the next task and, at a very late stage in construction it was learned that the main deck was to be planked in deal. It is always easier to plank decks before too much detail is applied to the model and before the superstructure is completed but in this case such was not possible. Thankfully the area concerned was quite small. To simulate the deal, thin birch

A first-prize winning model of the schooner Bluenose *passing between buoys at the National regatta held at Doncaster in 1994.*

plywood was cut into 6mm wide strips with a craft knife, the edges were lightly sanded smooth and then run down with a black, felt-tipped marking pen to simulate the caulking. Each plank was laid using white PVA adhesive and once the deck was completed the whole area was lightly sanded before applying three coats of matt varnish. It was interesting to see the full-size deck being laid over the steel decking, each plank was bolted down through deeply cut holes in the planks. The holes were filled with dowels of deal glued in place, the caulking was done in the traditional manner using caulking tools which must have been some years old and the only modern part of the operation was that the pitch used was of cold and modern chemical composition.

All during the currency of the building work at the shipyard, the owner visited at regular intervals and, quite often altered plans to suit his personal needs. This led to some problems with the model, particularly as the owner was kept in the dark regarding the model which was to be given to him as a surprise on the naming day. There were a couple of occasions when a visit to the yard was cancelled because it coincided with his visit. Suffice to say the model work proceeded with few interruptions and making and fitting of the deck furniture was done next.

Bollards fashioned from styrene sheet and knitting needle rod were made to match the drawings and photographs. Once completed they were mounted on a strip of plywood using double-sided adhesive tape and spray painted matt white. Spray painting in this way ensures a consistent finish and also making the fitting in advance allows adequate drying time before it is needed. The fairleads for this ship were formed within the ship's rails, the lower bars of the rails were cut and bent

to shape and in the space thus created, the fairleads were fitted and the lower bars welded to them. Initially, this seemed to be a difficult task but once the first was made it was very easy to repeat the exercise for the remaining four. Mushroom and tank vents were made from the ubiquitous knitting needle and fitted in place after being painted. Pipes with valves, painted red for fire service, were made from scraps of styrene tube and rod. Handwheels of etched brass completed the valves which were fitted to the forward bulkhead of the bridge unit. Pond boards made from sheet styrene were fitted between the bridge and the winch to create a pond in which the scallops could be sorted. Such ponds are needed as the scallops could easily be washed overboard through the relief ports. Finally the ship's name, port of registry and registration number and letters were applied using rub-down lettering; this lettering was sealed with a couple of coats of matt varnish from the Humbrol range. The whole hull was examined for any possible damage and the paintwork was carefully checked. The white and gold lines adorning the hull were applied using fine lining strips purchased from Westbourne Model Centre. The coach lines available from car accessory dealers can be used but they are not so fine and are harder to apply round small curves.

To mount the model in its display case two mahogany frames were made to simulate the timber baulks used when the ship was in dry dock. These were glued to the base of the display case and the model was, in turn, glued to the frames. A brass plate inscribed with the legend required by the shipyard was mounted in the case and the completed model was delivered to the shipyard two days before the full-size ship was handed to her owner. In all the project had been different but very enjoyable.

Chapter 15   General notes, hulls and hull building

Each ship design relies upon a specific hull form and most naval architects design their hulls to suit the workload that the ship is geared to do. Some will be outfitted with bulbous bow sections, some with very slender bow sections. Some will be beamy where the ratio of length to beam is very low so that the ship will handle heavy seas without shipping too much water, and others will be quite slender and designed to cut through the water in the manner of a destroyer. All will most probably be designed on a computer and have computer-generated section lines and drawings. Frequently the hull form will be modelled and tank-tested to ensure that it will be suitable for its duty.

All new ships without exception will be fitted with engines that have adequate power to propel the ship at economic and sensible speed, and also to be able to trawl and/or handle the nets. This is not so easy a decision to take - it is sometimes necessary to sacrifice speed for bollard pull - but it is essential to reach a compromise that will ensure the ship has the ability to make money and to recover the outlay needed to build it with a profit figure overall. In the early days of the drifter and trawler the hull forms used were taken from the sailing ships that were their precedents, with hulls being modified internally to accommodate boiler

Deck planking being laid over the steel deck of Academus.

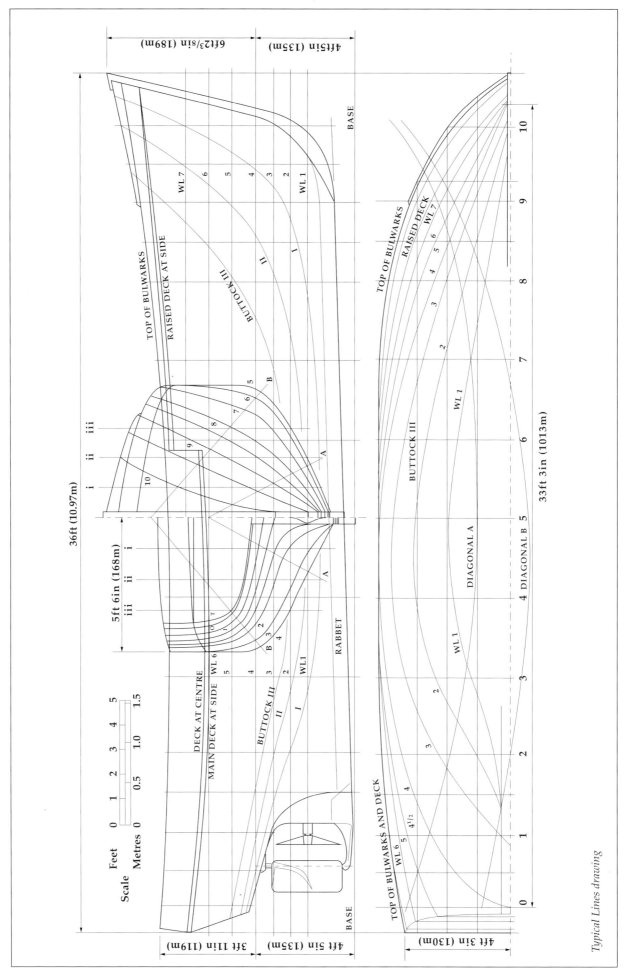

Typical Lines drawing

Deck planking completed round the fish hatch of Academus. *Note the wood dowels covering holding down bolts.*

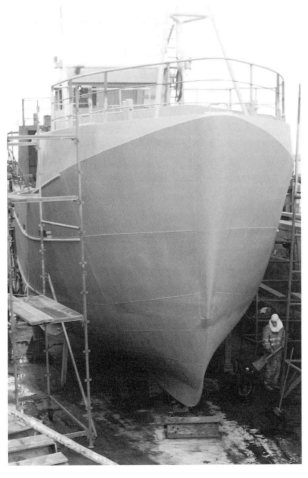

Academus in dry dock with hull painting in progress.

and engines. It was soon realised that the power plants available could work much more efficiently if the ship's hull were to be shaped to reduce the braking effect of the water and allow the ship to proceed more easily.

Thus the variety of hull shapes that we see today has been developed over the years. The drawings accompanying this chapter illustrate a number of hull forms. As they are typical drawings they will be of interest to those who wish to build models from scratch. The kit builder really has no need for line drawings as very few kits today require the modeller to build up plank-on-frame hulls. Most kits include a ready-made hull, in either grp or ABS plastic. To build a plank-on-frame or bread-and-butter type hull is, however, a satisfying process. It is delightful to see the shape of the ship slowly appear as the planks are laid or the bread is planed and the end product is one of which the builder can be justly proud. There exist today, a number of informed volumes available to the model ship-builder that describe in detail the methods of building a ship's hull from timber or, indeed, many other materials (see Model Ships from Scratch by Scott Robertson published by Nexus Special Interests). There is little point therefore in repeating such descriptions here although a few points may not be amiss.

Academus *showing the finished paintwork.*

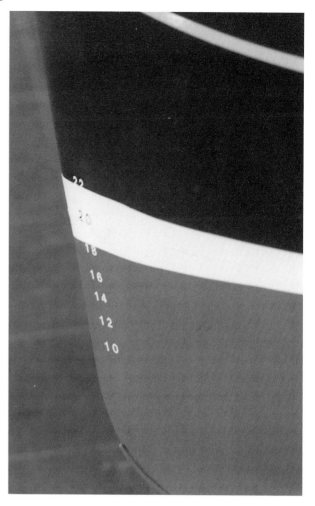

The bow of Academus *showing depth marks applied using Letraset rub-down figures.*

When laying planks over frames to make a plank-on-frame hull, use for preference small brass pins as they do not need to be subsequently removed or punched down; the soft brass sands away as easily as does the timber and no pin holes are left needing filler. Always fit planks to alternate sides of the hull and never to one side at a time - the latter method will surely lead to a hull out of true and the end result will be the need to destroy the work and start again. It is best to lay two or three planks each side of the model per session and allow the glue to set overnight before laying the next few at the next session. Some builders prefer to start laying the hull planks at deck level and work down to the keel, some prefer to start at the keel and work upwards; there appears to be no advantage with either method as long as all planks are laid with care and firmly glued one to another.

Regarding hulls built by the bread-and-butter method, it is essential that the 'butter' (glue) covers the whole glue area of each plank and that all planks are held under weights or in clamps until the glue cures before making any attempt to dress the outer shapes. The initial shaping of a bread-and-butter hull can be carried out with a good plane or spokeshave to remove quite large quantities of timber, but once the roughing out work has been done then shaping can only be done sensibly

with sandpaper and scraper. It is also vital to make use of a set of templates giving the hull shape at various frame stations - it is not possible to make an accurate hull by eye alone, templates are the only way you can be sure that the work is done correctly. Templates are easily prepared using the frame stations of the line drawings as guides; thin card, styrene sheet or thin plywood are all suitable material from which to cut such templates. Ensure that each is clearly marked at the line of the keel and at the main deck and devise a means of holding the template to the work so that it is always in the same position - in this way you can see whether more sanding is needed or where slight depressions need to be filled first.

With both types of hull, final finishing using progressively finer grades of sandpaper or similar abrasive cloth needs to be done by hand with the abrasive mounted on a block and not carried in the hand. Only by using a block will high spots be removed; when the paper is handheld the high spots continue into smoother and smoother places but still stay high. A good quality filler is a must for coating the hull and filling minor

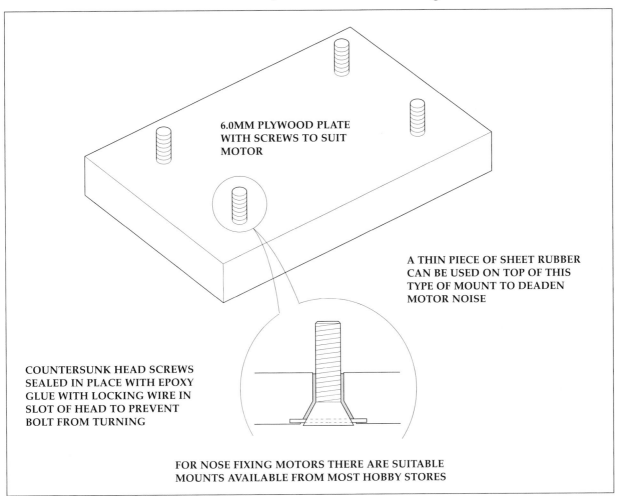

6.0MM PLYWOOD PLATE WITH SCREWS TO SUIT MOTOR

A THIN PIECE OF SHEET RUBBER CAN BE USED ON TOP OF THIS TYPE OF MOUNT TO DEADEN MOTOR NOISE

COUNTERSUNK HEAD SCREWS SEALED IN PLACE WITH EPOXY GLUE WITH LOCKING WIRE IN SLOT OF HEAD TO PREVENT BOLT FROM TURNING

FOR NOSE FIXING MOTORS THERE ARE SUITABLE MOUNTS AVAILABLE FROM MOST HOBBY STORES

Suggested method of making a mounting for an electric motor

depressions and marks. Do not be tempted by the cheap alternative fillers so often advertised at big DIY stores. Good filler is not cheap and cheap filler is not suitable for marine modelling. Once the hull has been made and is acceptable then the work of building the model can proceed as previously described.

It is possible to use the carefully made timber hull as a plug from which a mould can be made and in which subsequent identical hulls can be laid up using grp. You can do all of this work in the workshop but it is a fairly long process, the chemicals are strong smelling and unpleasant and the workshop needs to be conditioned to a temperature of at least 20 degrees C in order to permit the resins to cure correctly. The process of first making a mould and then producing hulls in grp has been described frequently in recent years in the model magazines. Almost all the major suppliers of the resins, glass cloth etc. that are needed for the work, provide data and instruction sheets for the user. The process is simple but also it is not one to be attempted in the domestic kitchen or even the garage unless the space is suitably heated and ventilated. Making grp hulls is probably best left to be tackled on warm, sunny days out of doors in

the garden or yard. It is a fact, of course, that most pre-made hulls found in kits are made from grp resin and glass fibre. A point well worthy of note is that grp hulls produced for the standard model ship kit are made from polyester resins and there are very few made with any other. Hulls made for very high speed, IC-engined models are more usually made from epoxy resins and with carbon fibre or Kevlar. Similarly model racing yachts use epoxy resin and carbon fibre hulls most frequently. These should not be confused and you will find that polyester resin material is much easier to find and buy than the other more expensive materials. Furthermore, using polyester resin as an adhesive to secure timber strips to the grp hull is much more likely to effect a good bond than using epoxy resin adhesive. The polyester resin gelcoat used to give the model hull a fine finish is thixotropic and therefore tends not to run down vertical surfaces, thus it is very suitable for use as an adhesive relative to the hull. Resin gelcoat or lay-up resin is not suitable for general use as an adhesive but it will bond materials to the grp hull quite well.

Having built the model ship hull and dressed it to a fine surface finish the question of how to pro-

A detail shot of the model winch constructed from timber, styrene and wire for Academus.

ceed comes next. Here there are two schools of thought: on the one hand the hull can be primed, the waterline marked off and the final finish paint can be applied, on the other hand work can proceed to fit propeller shafts, rudder etc., and the drive equipment. In the first instance, once the painting has been done it will be necessary to protect the hull from any form of knock, scrape etc., which may damage the paint. It will also be necessary to wait at least 14 days to allow the volatiles in the paint to evaporate and the paint to fully harden before subjecting the hull to further stress. In the second instance any work done inside the hull on drive equipment and radio gear will need to be protected when hull painting is carried out or the equipment will need to be removed to permit further work to be done.

Fitting drive gear

In all probability the second instance is wiser the way to go, drilling holes for propeller shaft(s) and rudder stocks, fitting bilge keels, cutting away the hull and fitting anchor boxes, fitting rubbing strips and bulwarks are all best done before the hull is painted. Fitting after painting will, almost invariably, damage the paint finish. Think carefully about this before proceeding further. The question of fitting drive equipment is also one to be

considered - it is much easier to fit motors, couplings and shafts into the hull before the decks are fitted than afterwards. Lining up shaft, coupling and motor shaft is a task that requires great care. Using a single coupling it is essential to ensure that the three units are completely in line in all directions if overloading the motor is to be avoided. With a double coupling it is possible to allow a slight misalignment in one direction only but not in two directions. A sensitive ammeter in series with the motor will show the lowest reading when the motor and shaft assembly is in line and this is the way to proceed (see earlier chapters).

How the shaft(s) should be mounted is another matter for serious consideration. In the hull of the single screw ship there is little to concern the modeller except that most hulls are waisted at the stern (very narrow) and therefore in order to get sufficient space in which to fit the motor; the shaft needs to be a long one. Many single screw ships have propeller shafts which lie almost parallel to the keel and leave insufficient space underneath to allow the motor to sit down low enough. If it is necessary to raise the inboard end of the shaft to give clearance for the motor mounting then the longer the shaft the smaller the angle of line of the shaft. When twin shafts are needed then they obviously exit the hull on either side of the keel at

107

a reasonable distance from it. Here too, it is necessary to assess the position of the motor or engine in order to allow space for the mounting. Always keep propeller shafts as low as possible and, to ensure rigidity for the inner shaft, always fit a support at the inboard end of the shaft close to the coupling location. The shaft support can be made from scrap of plywood or timber and sealed to the outer casing of the shaft with epoxy or similar adhesive.

The support for the motor or engine needs to be made with care; many modellers make a simple cradle and secure the motor in the cradle with rubber bands. This method is fine for a very small model but is totally unsuitable for a large and heavy tug or similar ship. One must bear in mind that the lake in the local park, while used regularly by the local model boat club, is generally far from being free of detritus. It is very easy to get weed wrapped round a propeller or a piece of plastic bag or string and the net result would be, were the method above to be adopted, that the motor would be thrown out of the mounting and the hull would be damaged by the blow. It is much safer to have the motor or engine bolted down to a suitable bed plate fastened firmly into the hull and to ensure that suitable fuses are used to protect the motor should the propeller become seized. The sketches given here show some methods of making motor mountings that are secure yet allow the motor to be removed easily.

It is always wise to give the inside gubbins of the model the same degree of care that you give to the outside. Although it is the outside of the model that is seen and judged at a regatta, the inside is the bit that does the driving and care within will avoid the breakdown on the pond that so often happens at the wrong time. Once more the watchword must be quality in preference to price when choosing drive and radio equipment. The cheap motor may work quite well for a season but will rarely last for long, the cheap shaft will almost certainly lack a suitable lubricating point or a place to fit one and the cheap radio will rarely do all it is cracked up to do. Consider the overall cost of the model carefully. For example, a kit costs £200.00 and takes some 300 hours to construct and bring to a state when it can be sailed on the pond. The cost per hour at that point is only 0.66 pence, but if you then add the cost of radio, batteries, single motor and speed controller, all of good quality, then a further £120.00 would be added and the cost per hour will rise to just over £1.00 per hour. This rates as very cheap entertainment even though the costs allowed are not the cheapest that could be found. It is thus very sensible to look at all the costs in

this way - no hobby is without cost but some are considerably cheaper than others.

Fitting out the model hull

The following few suggestions show how the installation of equipment into the hull is best carried out:

Fitting the rod drive from the servo horn to the rudder tiller is best done using proprietary clevis forks or similar fittings, such units use rod which is threaded at one end allowing a degree of linear adjustment thus ensuring that the movement is free.

Fitting servo units properly by using the rubber bushes and brass inserts correctly and using the screws provided to fasten the servos down ensures that they remain reasonably rigid and yet have a small movement allowance through the bushes to absorb shocks. Using adhesive soft plastic mounts to secure servo units is alright where the servo has little more than its own turning movement to contend with but not good enough where it is controlling a rudder - even a fairly light rudder.

Fitting sealed lead acid batteries and radio battery packs into the hull also needs care. Initially they should be located when the hull is floated in a bath so that the best position for the weight can be assessed. Following such tests a suitable frame should be built into the hull in which the battery(ies) can be placed and held so that they do not move relative to movement of the hull. Should a battery shift in the hull when it is underway on the pond then the hull could be so affected that water could enter and sink it. Most sealed lead acid batteries are quite heavy and can contribute to the ballast needed to float the model correctly. Small battery packs of nicad or similar units are, in general, reasonably light in weight and unlikely to affect the models trim unduly unless, of course, the model is very small.

All 'dirty' wiring should be kept to one side of a model and all 'clean' wiring should be kept to the other. So-called dirty wiring is that which carries current from the battery(ies) through to the speed controllers and then to the drive motors. Clean wiring is that carrying radio signals from radio receiver to servos and R/C switchgear. It is essential that the two wiring systems are kept apart to avoid any radio interference from the dirty wires.

Careful tests carried out at set distances between model and radio transmitter will soon indicate whether suppression equipment needs to be fitted across the motor terminals. Packs of suitable suppressers and capacitors etc. are available from specialist model and radio shops; these are easy to fit although they do have to be soldered in place.

It is wise to very carefully check the whole of the equipment fitted inside the hull and to have a test run in the bath or garden pond before proceeding to lay decks etc.

Provision should be made for the later fitting of lighting, sound, smoke etc., before decks are laid too. It is often very difficult to fit small wires inside a hull when the deck has been fitted. It is also wise to provide a suitable run for the radio receiver aerial at an early stage of construction, such aerial wires should not be cut to shorter lengths as such cutting will reduce the signal strength to the receiver. If the aerial wire is too long to be comfortably fitted round the perimeter of the hull or a suitable superstructure then it should be wrapped round a short piece of dowel which, in turn, should be fixed to a suitable place in the hull. If it is necessary to make the receiver aerial detachable to suit a given type of deckhouse, a banana pattern plug and socket can be used to interconnect the two parts and to give the overall length supplied by the makers.

Make absolutely certain that access is maintained close to the radio receiver to allow for changing the crystals of the radio equipment. A spare set of different frequency crystals will allow one to sail more easily and to change a crystal in the outfit

takes but a few seconds assuming that access to the receiver is easy.

Finally there will be those who wish to fit auxiliary features and control them remotely and provision for installing such equipment needs also to be done at an early stage in the construction. To summarise it is very necessary for the model builder, whether building a kit or working from raw materials from scratch, to set out a scheme or schedule of operation or a sequence of building so that small and silly errors can be avoided and so that a part is not fitted out of sequence that causes access for other parts to become constricted. Think carefully - measure twice and cut once - and use a good steel rule with a cutting mat for safe cutting of thin plywood and styrene. Always try to be one step ahead, and to note those places on the model that need to be primed and painted before other parts are added and make access impossible. When building the deckhouse or superstructures consider the effect of leaving the inside of the model without detail. If windows or portlights are large then the interior will be visible even from a short distance away and you need to show some form of furniture and decor to avoid a plain blank. If the portlights are small then sometimes it is best to colour the interior behind black as this is nondescript and less likely to become too obvious.

You can see from these pages that there is scope for all sorts of innovations and ideas but they are best carried out with a degree of care if the idea or innovational piece is not to become too obtrusive.

Chapter 16 Drawings, scales, fittings and ballasting

Reading through the model magazines available from the newsagents or on subscription today, you will find many manufacturers offering pre-formed hulls, usually of grp construction, together with drawings to allow you to complete a ship model without the need to build a hull. This is often the only way you can find a hull for a specific ship model that is not made as a full kit and yet does remove some of the research and waiting that could well be the case for a more unusual ship. These hulls are produced in small quantities by the specialist maker where there is a small demand but not one large enough to justify the production of a full kit.

Sometimes such hulls can be found to accompany drawings available from the plans services. Often the hull and drawings have been produced by a professional model maker where he/she needed a hull in grp for a particular client and where the cost of having a single hull made is thus offset by passing the details to the hull maker, who can then market a small quantity and recover the high cost of production mould making.

Building a model using such facilities is just as rewarding and saves considerable time by removing the hull-making part of the job. As previously mentioned, quite a number of grp hulls can spread open at deck level (see Chapter 11 for techniques to remedy this) and it is always wise to check the beam of the hull at deck level to ensure accuracy.

Detail of the fish hatch, hinges and cover on Academus.

The tank vent with cover and hand pump in pipework on a full-size ship.

Before proceeding too far always check dimensions carefully as there is a tendency for copies of drawings to have slight errors upon reproduction so they should be used with care. Regretfully not all kit makers or hull producers provide drawings that are full size for the model or even of scale size. Drawings that are provided at, say, half the size of the hull or kit scale are easily used by doubling every measurement taken from the drawing before applying it to the model. Drawings that are to an unusual scale compared to that of the kit or hull need to used with greater care. A set of proportional dividers, available from some specialist model shops or from drawing office supply companies, are of great value for increasing or decreasing dimensions from one drawing to another. These instruments have points at both ends. By setting the scale in the centre the points at one end, when placed over a given measurement, will set the points at the other end accurately to the increase or decrease needed for the work in hand i.e. setting the scale at 2 would allow the points at one end set to 10mm to provide the points at the other end to read 20mm thereby doubling the measurement. Each time the points at one end read from the drawing, the points at the other end would indicate double until the scale is reset. Such dividers are however expensive, and it is possible that they could be an item purchased by a club or group to be available at a small charge for members when needed.

The ship modeller who seeks to enter models into competition, especially those competitions that include examination of the model for quality of work etc., needs always to be sure that the work is done accurately. It is essential that the measuring instruments used are accurate - good stainless steel rules are not expensive and are worth investing in. Measurements should be taken, not from the extreme end of the rule but from a point a short way up the scale. The end of the rule is easily damaged and the first small scale is almost certain to be slightly under the correct size. By starting to measure at 10mm from the end of the rule only means that 10mm must be added to each dimension taken but these measurements will be that little more accurate.

Other measuring instruments should also be used with care. Spring bow and plain dividers are very useful for transferring measurements from drawing to work material. Bear in mind too the thickness of the pencil point when drawing lines upon styrene or thin plywood; this pencil line can be a full 1.0mm thick or more and this can make a difference to the construction of a model. If 1.0mm is repeated over 10 measurements along the length of a superstructure that is but 200mm long it will be 10mm too long when tried on the model deck. The importance of repeatedly checking dimensions and measurements cannot be over-emphasised because compounding errors will certainly lead to serious problems eventually.

Building model deck machinery when working from scale drawings can often give rise to problems, but here the accuracy of measurements can

A small davit with rope blocks carrying a large rubber fender for the bunkering tanker Rix Harrier.

sometimes lead to difficulties. A winch which, in scale, is only 40mm long x 30mm deep and 25mm tall is very small and you cannot expect to be 100% accurate when making such things as handwheel spindles and similar shafts for such a small size. To ensure that they can be strong enough to support even a light etched brass handwheel, the spindle will need to be bigger in diameter that the scale suggests. Such small inaccuracies are to be expected and allowed for. It is the larger and more glaringly obvious inaccuracies which must be avoided.

Today it is possible to buy from a range of fittings and castings too great for the average model shop to hold more than a limited selection. These fittings and castings are being produced by makers from all over the world, a significant contrast to the situation just twenty years ago when the range of ready-made fittings for the model ship was small, restricted and, in general, of poor scale reproduction. There is little need for the modeller today to make more than a few specialised parts unless the model being built is to an unusual scale. Some samples of fittings currently available are shown in the photographs. as are some fittings that have needed to be specially built for specific models.

If you should find that the ship of your choice needs a number of fittings, such as bollards for example, but that such fittings are not available from the model trade, it is possible to produce a simple master and to hand-cast repeats in white

A port side view of a full-size vessel showing bollards, pipes and large fender.

metal with a time-saving advantage. Ten bollards would take a fair while to make and get exactly alike whereas one made in styrene or similar material, but made with great care and accuracy, can be used as a master from which a silicon rubber mould can be made and in which replicas can be cast in white metal. Hand-casting in white metal or casting resin is within the ability of most ship modellers and is a relatively easy task if tackled sensibly. It must be borne in mind that you will be working with hot molten metal and thus proper precautions need to be taken. The materials necessary for making the moulds and the metals for casting therein can be bought quite reasonably from specialist suppliers who advertise regularly in the model press. Trylon Ltd (see Appendix 2), can provide small quantities of the material and a detailed instruction leaflet to allow the model maker to try out the system before investing in larger quantities of material. In the same way as white metal casting is carried out, so can casting be done in a suitable resin that has been catalysed. This has the advantage that the material is used cold but the casting-in resin requires longer times for curing than white metal does for setting. In both cases it is wise to carry out the work in the workshop or garage and away from the home and children. White metals are to some degree toxic and need, when hot, to be treated with respect as the gases are unpleasant and can, in concentration, be dangerous. There are so many processes used in hobbies that can be seen to be dangerous or odorous - chemicals used in photography, etching etc. are all unpleasant. Hooks used in fishing are dangerous; flying model aircraft can cause injuries etc. Hobbies are good leisure pursuits if followed with care and model boats are no exception.

The newcomer to model shipbuilding will find that the materials he or she needs cannot all be bought from one supplier, and information will be required as to the sources from which certain items or pieces can be obtained. To this end the appendices will be of some assistance but it is best, where possible, to seek out catalogues which not only provide data and prices but also illustrations. Regretfully not all catalogues give full illustrative data but they do generally advise of the scale of the parts. From the scale given you can generally determine the size of the part in question. Some catalogues will list, for example, stanchions of the single, two or three ball pattern and not give the scale but they will provide the overall height which frequently is sufficient to allow the correct item to be selected. Anchors are often logged in the same way by the length of the stock in preference to the scale. The main reason for this is quite simple - anchors and stanchions, bollards etc. are made to suit a given duty and not a given size of

Pipes and valves on the deck of a large ship - note the bolted covers to access hatches.

The forward deck of Rix Harrier *showing the anchor windlass, rope guides, Panama pots, tank vents etc.*

ship, i.e. one type of ship will carry single ball stanchions on top of the main bulwark rail and these will be quite small relative to the scale of the model. Similarly, a Hall anchor on one ship model at 1:50 scale may have a stock of 40mm long whereas a different ship to the same scale may carry an anchor having a stock of only 30mm long. The size of the anchor depends upon the size of the ship and thus the duty required of the anchor and its associated chain cable, all the sizes of which are laid down by the Board of Trade or the Classification Societies. It is not, therefore, possible for the model manufacturer to be precise regarding the sizes of some fittings.

Many other anomalies will present themselves as the modeller constructs the ship model. Why; for example, is one ship fitted with a steering wheel on the bridge while another is controlled by a simple joystick? This is quite often down to the personal requirements of the owner, particularly in the case of fishing vessels where the owner actually sails the ship as its master. As previously mentioned, the rudders of modern tugs or fishing vessels are usually controlled electro-hydraulically and remotely from the bridge as distinct from the earlier days of chain and rod operation from a wheel and gypsy. Such control can easily be done either by a joystick or by a steering wheel with little difference in cost. In the case of the tug, the rudder control can be repeated on the bridge wings so that the master can steer the ship from either bridge wing at will.

More and more frequently too, full remote control of engines both for direction and speed is done from the bridge leaving the engineer to attend to the running of the plant in preference to operating to the dictates of the engine-room telegraph. Such remote control of speed and direction is, today, more likely to control a variable pitch propeller allowing the main engine to be run at a constant and economical speed at all times. Of interest to the model shipbuilder, the variable pitch propeller is now available in model form at least in two standard sizes and at a cost which closely approximates that of a standard fixed blade propeller with an electronic speed controller. A worthwhile consideration if the prototype being followed is a ship fitted with a variable pitch unit.

There are some points that have yet to be clarified and the first concerns the weight of the ship and the provision of ballast. In the case of a tug for instance, ballast will probably be needed to bring the model down to its normal waterline and working position. Tugs are seen always at the same loading as they do not carry cargo or materials that will cause the vessel's depth in the water to vary. Fishing boats and cargo-carrying vessels, while provided with a clearly seen waterline and a Plimsoll line, are not always loaded down to the marks depending whether or not they are fully laden, empty or somewhere in between. It is not uncommon to see a fishing boat sailing to the grounds with her bow high out of the water indicating that she is unladen. Conversely the same ship returning from a fishing trip will be deep in the water if she has had a successful trip. The model builder must decide how to show the model on the water and be very careful that, when the model is ballasted, it does not lie incorrectly. Ships with engines aft are usually low in the water at the stern when sailing empty but high at the bow. Ships are never lower at the bow than at the stern.

Ballast is best applied using thin sheet lead such as would be used for flashing on a roof. This sheet lead can be bought in rolls from a builder's merchant or, if you are very lucky, as used scrap from friendly local builder. To permit the model to roll realistically the lead sheet should be fitted from the keel up each side of the hull and fixed firmly in place. There is one exception to this rule and that is if the model is very tender, i.e. it has a tendency to roll completely over when a list is applied. In this case the weight of ballast must be applied over the keel and low down in the hull. Place the model in a bath of water and apply the ballast in small pieces over the hull bottom until the ship lies correctly to your requirements; note the position of the loosely applied weights and mark the inside of the hull accordingly before taking the model out of the water. On the bench, shape the lead sheets to match the weight used for the floatation test and fix them up the sides of the hull from the keel. Tack the lead and re-float the model as a check that all is well - if all is correct seal the lead to the hull using silicon rubber sealant, polyester resin or epoxy. The silicon bath sealant is possibly the best method as, when necessary, the lead can be removed fairly easily. There will be occasions when the model being built requires a very large amount of weight which will make it difficult to carry. In this case it will be wise to consider making a series of frames within the hull into which blocks of lead can be placed after the model is floated on the lake thus allowing easier handling.

There have been some suggestions put to me regarding the possibility of ballasting the model using water in bottom tanks that could be flooded when the ship is placed on the pond and drained when it is removed. This has been given me a great deal of thought and, while it is a possibility if electric pumps and well-baffled tanks in the bottom of the hull are used, it is a matter which requires real care to be taken. Water sloshing back and forth in a hull will cause serious problems of stability if not in tanks which are baffled to prevent too much movement of the liquid. Ships carrying liquids in bulk do so in tanks which are quite small and designed to prevent too much movement of the liquid despite the movement of the ship in the water. To repeat this in a model is possible but, dependent upon the size of the model, can be quite difficult. Furthermore, the water tanks would need to be completely watertight to ensure that no water gets near the electrics of the model or a disastrous short circuit could occur. There are other means of ballasting the model - small pieces of any heavy material that can be sealed into the hull are suitable - but, whatever material is used, it is important to ensure that it is secured to the hull so that it cannot move about.

When you reach the stage of installing the deck machinery and fittings that are needed on all models you will quickly learn whether the model is going to be top heavy or not. A model that has a shallow draft and yet carries many white metal fittings on and above the main deck is almost certain to be tender. The worst sufferers from this condition are usually models of warships which are long and narrow and which carry a great deal of clutter on and above the main deck. This armament etc., if made in white metal or similar heavy-weight material, is going to make the model tender unless the ballast is placed immediately over the keel and with all the weight very low in the hull. In general, neither tug or fishing boat models suffer from this condition but it is one that needs to be assessed and dealt with before making the first visit to the lake. Check that once all the ballast has been fitted and is secure, when the model is deliberately heeled over to one side or the other it will return to the vertical sensibly and freely. This return, on a well-ballasted model, will be deliberate and without too much counter movement in the opposite direction. On a badly ballasted model with all the weight over the keel and low down, the model will return to the vertical with a rapid jerky movement. The latter condition cannot be avoided with a tender model, but it should be avoided wherever possible.

All merchant ships carry depth markings at bow and stern or on the stern quarter, including tugs. Modern marks are metric, in Arabic numerals and indicate the depth of the immersed hull in 200mm intervals. Earlier ships had depth marks in feet and were in Roman numerals on one side and Arabic on the other. When building the scale model take care to verify in which period the model is to be depicted and use the correct markings to suit. The Plimsoll line marks are to be found on either side of commercial ships at a point midway between the perpendiculars. Note that most tugs did not carry Plimsoll line marks and only a few fishing boats were so fitted, as the carrying capacity of both types of ship is very small relative to their gross tonnage there is no requirement for such marks insisted upon by the Classification Rules. However, in all cases it is wise to check whether such marks were made to the full-size ship.

There are many methods of finishing the model ship which make it unique to its builder. Working

functions such as navigation lights, fire monitors, smoke units, sound systems and windlasses etc., can be found on many models. These often show the creativity of the builder and many unusual methods of working such extras can be found. It is certainly pleasant to see a model showing working lights, smoke from the funnel and to hear the sound of healthy engines running as the model passes by. Ensure that the effects that you install are correct for the period of the prototype ship - it would be ludicrous to see a steam outline model and hear the sound of a multi-cylinder oil engine or to see a motor ship belching black smoke and steam. It is not impossible to see a motor ship with black smoke from the funnel but such smoke is rare and generally to be found only when the engine is first fired up or when it is working particularly hard and is in need of attention.

If you are given the chance to visit a working ship take note of the deck machinery - a few well-chosen questions to the crew will often give the data required. Note the size of winches and windlasses, bollards, fairleads etc., and also make note of the various sizes of blocks to be found in the rigging of the ship. Nothing is left to chance on the best-designed ships and all fittings will generally carry an allowance over that laid down by the surveyor from the Classification Society so that a small overload can be accommodated if necessary in an emergency. Do not forget that once the vessel is at sea there is no chance of stopping at the nearest garage to have a puncture repaired while you wait. The safety of the crew, the cargo and the ship is in the hands of the master and the condition of the ship. A poorly outfitted ship will certainly end up with problems requiring assistance - help at sea invokes the laws of salvage on the part of the salvager. Even though the survey requirements are high and such surveys are held every two years, some second-class parts can sometimes slip through the safety net and cause problems. The same high quality standards should equally be provided for the model so that it will not fail on the water under stringent running conditions. Use always the best that can be afforded - that is not to say buy high-priced timber, quite often an old wardrobe or dressing table that has been discarded will supply a stock of quality and well seasoned timber perfectly adequate for even the most strict modeller. But do examine all the items that you buy and be sure that what is purchased is up to the duty required of it and the best quality that can be afforded.

The photographs that accompany this chapter have been selected to aid you by showing details of both full-size machinery and well-modelled items of deck fittings.

Chapter 17 Navigation lights, lighting and operational features

The question of what method of drive to install was dealt with in Chapter 6 and the data given there applies equally to the model fishing vessel. It is rare to find a fishing boat fitted with twin screws, in fact, I can find no references to any so fitted. The most modern fishing vessels are more frequently fitted with Kort-type nozzles surrounding the propeller which, in some cases, are steerable. As previously mentioned, there is also a tendency to using the variable pitch propeller that is easily controlled from the bridge. The size of the model and the displacement of the hull will dictate the size of motor or engine to be fitted and it is necessary for you to consider this carefully - reference to the data provided in Chapter 6 will certainly help.

Navigation lights

The fishing boat is fitted with an array of navigation lights, the illumination of which indicates what the ship is doing so that other ships can be aware of the nets etc. and keep well clear. Many fishing vessels carry out their work during the early hours just before dawn when the fish rise to feed and the nets can spread to a considerable distance from the ship. For this reason other ships need to be made aware of the lie and distance of the nets to avoid problems. One of the sketches here illustrates the lights of the ship and the main mast, and gives details of what the showing of such lights will indicate to other vessels. Such indicating lights must not be confused with the normal navigation lights which are red to port, green to starboard, white at forward mast and white astern when the ship is underway. These lights are indicated on the drawing too.

In addition to those shown the fishing boat generally carries an extra mast, usually on the port side of the wheelhouse or bridge top, with three white lights at equal distances above each other. These lights indicate the fishing that is in progress and will indicate to others what is happening. The

boat will sometimes be lying and drifting to the line of nets, sometimes hauling a trawl, sometimes tending to a purse seine net or other duty and the combination of lights will show the duty. In daylight these lights are replaced usually by black balls run up the same mast. It is therefore necessary for you to check that the lights fitted to the model are exactly as those fitted to the full-size

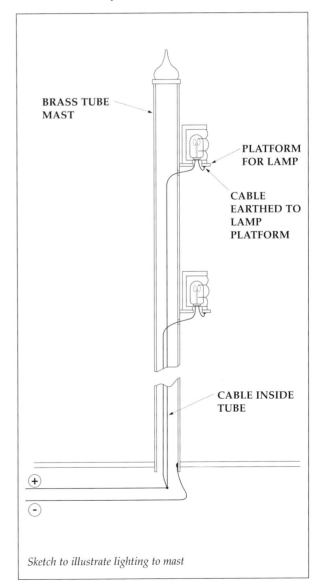

BRASS TUBE MAST

PLATFORM FOR LAMP

CABLE EARTHED TO LAMP PLATFORM

CABLE INSIDE TUBE

+

−

Sketch to illustrate lighting to mast

ship. If the model is to be sailed at a night-time regatta then it is only necessary for it to show the port and starboard red and green, and the fore and aft white lights as it is most unlikely that it will actually be fishing. If; however, the model is night sailing and dressed overall for a special occasion then all the lights on board would be lit at the same time.

It is quite possible for you to fit working lights to the model although those models built to very small scales do pose problems here. Many kit makers and manufacturers of model ship fittings offer lamps fitted with suitable operating light bulbs. These vary in voltage, some being 3, some 6 and some 12 volts and, of course, it is necessary to select the voltage you require and ensure that all lamps are to the same voltage. There is a distinct move today to the use of the light-emitting diode (LED) which has a much longer life than the simple filament lamp but, until very recently, it was not possible to obtain LEDs with a white light and yellow had to be used. A white light LED has recently become available but, at the time of writing, these are almost ten times the cost of the coloured units.

Where masts are constructed from brass tube it is an easy matter to wire up the lights by using the brass tube as the negative wire and feeding single positive wires to each lamp as illustrated in the sketch here. If the mast or fitting for the lamp is of styrene tube or similar non-conductive material then it will be necessary to run two wires to each lamp. When using filament lamps it is wise to provide current at slightly less than the rated current of the lamp as this will extend the life of the filament and lead to fewer failures. For example, if the light bulbs are all rated at 12 volts, by providing a 10-volt supply there will be no appreciable reduction in brightness but there will be a lengthened bulb life. In the same way 6 volts fed at 4.8 volts will have the same effect.

There are many types and sizes of filament lamps and LEDs on the market, generally available from your local model shop. Where the fitting is made to suit the model, care is needed to fit the correct size of lamp so that replacement can be easily effected when required. It is also necessary to route wires so that they are hidden from view and to fit switches and battery packs where they are accessible but hidden. Some ships' fittings lend themselves to adaptation to form switches to allow operation without the need to remove superstructures and you will, no doubt, be able to devise some simple form of switch using a deck fitting. Do remember to ensure that such switches will not become immersed in water resulting in a short circuit.

A neatly cast and painted binnacle for a model tug.

For the very small scale model and, perhaps, even some of the larger models it is possible to use fibre optic material to give illumination to lights from a central source. This flexible fibre rod is easily fastened to the ship's sides and to the walls of cabins etc. where it can feed to the location needed for the light. The actual lamp will need to carry a coloured lens if the lamp is, say, the port or starboard unit as the point of the fibre optic rod being very small, cannot easily be coloured. The light source with its shield and fitting to take the fibre optic elements can be located within the superstructure or hull of the model and the lamp fed from either a separate battery or from the main drive battery. Unless the fibre optic cable is damaged, light will not leak from it and it is a particularly feasible method of illuminating a small model. Maplins and other specialist suppliers offer kits from which to make suitable fibre optic systems at a reasonable cost - certainly there is little difference between the fibre optic system and the filament lamp system.

With all illumination systems it is essential to ensure that light from navigation lamps does not leak away and that the direction of the light is correctly placed. Lights which are needed to provide illumination over a given arc, as laid down by the Classification Societies, should be so arranged on the model for realism. When correctly installed and lit, an illuminated model sailing in the evening is a pleasurable sight. Coupling illumination with other functions can frequently lift a mundane model onto a much higher plane.
As has been stated many times before it is always wise to carry out each section of the work with

Twin roller fairleads on the stern trawler Glenrose 1.

care. Wiring to the model ship's lights can be carried out using fine single or multi-core cable, but such cable should be well jointed and well secured to the hull or superstructure. Joints should be soldered and insulated or the cables led to jointing strips. Soldered joints insulated using shrinkwrap sleeving are an excellent way to go. Shrinkwrap in many colours and in sizes to suit most cable sizes is available from many sources (see Appendix 2). It is easy to use requiring only moderate heat to shrink the sleeving really tight - a lit match can provide all the heat needed to shrink the sleeves but this method tends to leave a sooty deposit on the sleeve. The shank of a hot soldering iron or the heat from a pencil torch applied carefully will shrink the sleeving neatly and leave no marks. Blu Tack can be used to hold small cables in place but it is best to use one of the proprietary adhesive clips that can be bought from radio stores and some model shops for a small sum.

Always secure cables neatly and, where possible, couple cables together to form a wiring harness or loom. It is possible to buy a spiral wrapping of, usually, clear plastic which can be used to bind cables together and to make the harness tidy. If the cable runs are carried out using different coloured cables then it is easy to trace each one should a fault occur. If using coloured cables is not possible then each cable should be tagged, at regular intervals, with a number or sign and a note should be kept of the numbering or marking system. Failure adequately to identify cables can

cause a great deal of trouble at the pondside if a fault becomes apparent and the cables leading to the fault cannot be traced. If the wiring of the model covers only a single motor, speed controller and steering servo from a two-channel radio and a single main battery then there are very few wires involved. But if the model has operating lights, a fire monitor, a sound system, twin screws, two motors, a bow thruster and an operating radar unit then there will be a considerable number of cables and a wiring diagram covering all the runs is to be considered as essential. A typical wiring diagram is given in one of the sketches and there is no reason why a similar diagram should not be prepared for any model. The newcomer to model shipbuilding will be well advised to make simple wiring diagrams for his/her models from the very beginning and even for simple models. This will lead to clearer understanding of wiring and to easier building and cabling for larger and more complex models.

Sound systems

Many models today are fitted out with sound systems, in the first instance generally to provide engine sound. Some models will have a siren sound too and others will go further and have music. One item that needs to be located most carefully for the sound system is the loudspeaker. A good loudspeaker needs to be securely mounted on what is known as a baffle board, i.e. a timber or plywood board with a suitably sized hole to which

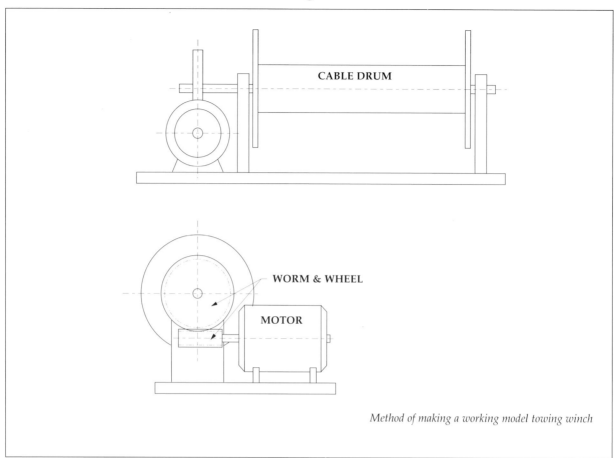

CABLE DRUM

WORM & WHEEL

MOTOR

Method of making a working model towing winch

the speaker can be bolted. The hole in the board should be equivalent to the diameter of the vibrating cone of the speaker. Many speakers today come with transparent plastic covers which help to render the speaker less prone to problems from damp atmosphere. The speaker for the model must be matched to the sound unit, although a speaker of 8 ohms impedance would seem to be the norm. Above all, the speaker and its mounting board must be firmly attached to the hull or superstructure of the model and the model needs to have a clear or a number of clear holes somewhere high up in the deck housing to allow the sound to exit without being muffled. One means of ensuring that the sound has a clear field is to place the speaker in the floor of the bridge and leave a number of bridge windows open. Such openings need to be high to prevent ingress of water when the model is underway in poor conditions. A fine cloth cover to the speaker where it is mounted in the floor of the bridge can be coloured to simulate the bridge flooring and thus hide the speaker. The sound unit itself can be fitted in any suitable place within the hull. A number of manufacturers make sound systems and some provide such units in kit form thereby lowering the costs. Sometimes articles on making sound systems from scratch appear in the model press - most large towns have branches of Maplins or Tandy or similar radio component companies where the parts needed for sound units can be found.

There is little doubt that the sound of a motor ship running close to shore with the sound varying with the speed of the model, does cause the onlooker to see the model much more clearly and frequently to ask questions and evince interest in the hobby. Those model boaters who are club members will almost invariably be courteous and answer these questions sensibly to encourage the questioner to join and take part in the club activities and to start a worthwhile hobby such as this.

Operating features

Many modellers, especially those whose skill has advanced beyond the small and two-channel controlled model, seek to enhance their ships with operating features such as working anchors, operating radar, working cranes etc. Some manufacturers offer kits that include ships with working daughter boats that can be released from the parent ship, sailed and returned and all under radio control. Although such daughter boats would not apply to the tug or fishing vessel some of the functions could be fitted to either. Nobody, to my knowledge, has yet fitted a model fishing boat with working trawl nets or nets of any kind that work but that, perhaps, is but a short while away. Maybe one day some bright model boater will come and scoop your goldfish from the pond with a fine model fishing boat under multi-channel radio control!

The name and registration number applied to the almost completed model of Academus.

There are other sections of the model tug or fishing vessel where the ingenuity of the builder can be brought to bear. Most of the large modern tugs use a winch for towing duty in preference to a hook and such winches can be made to operate if built in simple form. To operate such a winch it is necessary to use a channel of the radio control system and thus a system with six or seven channels is possibly required where more than just control of drives and rudder is needed. One method of building and driving a model winch is shown in the accompanying sketches; here it is essential to use gears to give the appropriately slow running of the winch. Using a worm drive for reduction has one distinct advantage in that the winch will not release its load when the power is taken off. Under radio control it is thus possible to reduce or lengthen the tow rope to allow more accurate control of the tow.

In the same way it is possible to make and fit a working anchor system. In this case it is probably best to install the moving parts of the system below the forward deck and have a purely cosmetic windlass on the fore deck. The anchor cable can be led over the dummy windlass and down to the operating drum mounted below. To run the anchor up and down successfully will be dependent upon fitting an anchor of fairly weighty construction, one that will freely run down under its own weight. The length of chain cable fitted will be dictated by the size of the drum on which it is wound. It is obviously not sensible to expect a model anchor to hold in the material at the bottom of a pond or even to reach the pond bottom, but the action will give realism to the operating model.

With the fishing boat you will find a number of winches that can be made to operate (possibly swinging) derricks and lifting a crate or similar cargo. The anchor can be made to work in the same way as for the tug above. Some fishing vessels carry hydraulic cranes with net guide drums etc. and there is possibly some means of making the hydraulic crane work. Swinging the crane round is easily done with a gear system from a small motor but making the rams that lift the crane arm work will need a more sophisticated control. There is the possibility of using toothed rod driven by a small gear but concealing this in the body of the crane would be difficult. Some bright modeller with a small lathe will no doubt, one day, make a set of fully working rams using fine oil and a pump but that is beyond the scope of this book.

Soldering

Electronics projects easily cope with flashing lights, searchlights and the operation thereof and there are often articles with full working drawings and diagrams in the model press covering such projects (see also Electronic Projects for Model Boats by Ken Ginn published by Nexus Special Interests). All that is required in the way of skill is in the efficient use of a soldering iron. Soft soldering is an easy job to do when tackled with care, however it should be remembered that when soldering cleanliness is of paramount importance. All parts to be joined need to be clean and free from grease or other contamination. Once cleaned, the parts should be lightly coated with flux - Fluxite paste is best for electrical work - and then, with an iron which is clean and well coated with solder, the two parts should be held together and heated. A small bead of solder applied to the heated parts and iron will run into the joint and show a bright silver line of solder. The iron should then be removed and the joint allowed to cool when it will be found to be solid. When soldering parts to a circuit board for an electronic control unit ensure that the board tracks, where working, are clean and use a suitable cored solder to make the joint. Cored solder carries flux inside the solder wire to make the jointing easy. The range of solders available to the model maker is quite extensive and it is possible to get solder in various temperature ranges to allow making a number of joints close to each other without the heat melting the first. Carrs Solders, which are held in stock by a number of specialist suppliers such as Squires (see Appendix 2), provide details and a range of fluxes for many varied solders and soldering aids.

There will come, at some time, the need to make joints in metals such as copper and brass that will stand up to heavy use and wear. For this duty it is necessary to use hard soldering (silver soldering) or brazing. The easier of these two options is silver soldering. Like soft soldering, cleanliness is next to Godliness and must be the watchword. For hard soldering you need a blowlamp, silver solder and flux. The solder can be bought in thin rods, thin sheet or stick form from good, specialist model shops or tool stores. The best for modelling use is generally the thin rod form which is to be found in lengths of about 15 inches or 400mm. A large firebrick will be needed as a hearth upon which to carry out the work and it is possible to buy a vermiculite block which is ideal for holding parts to be silver soldered. Pins can be inserted into the vermiculite to hold small parts firmly while they are being soldered. Most gas blowlamps have a range of nozzles permitting various sizes of flames to be used and the size needed for silver soldering is dictated by the size of the workpieces. Small pieces that have to be joined will only require a small flame to provide adequate heat, larger pieces will need larger flames.

The cleaned parts to be joined should be coated with the silver solder flux, usually Borax powder mixed with a little water to a paste of thick cream consistency, and fixed together in some way upon the firebrick and/or vermiculite block. The flame should then be played upon the parts until they become dull red when it will be found that a small bead of silver solder placed on the joint will run in and show a bright silver line all round. If necessary a little more solder can be applied, but only enough to show all round the joint is adequate. The piece should be thoroughly washed in hot water and scrubbed to remove any remaining flux after which it is ready for use.

Soldering with either soft solder or with silver solder is not a difficult task if the simple rules are observed. Make sure the parts to be joined are cleaned and grease-free before applying the flux. Note that your fingers are greasy even if you think they are not and cleaned parts should not be handled in the fingers but with tweezers, pliers and with the parts protected with clean cloth or paper

towels. Apply the heat, either with an iron for soft solder or with a blowlamp for hard or soft solder, until the solder when touched to the parts runs freely into the joint. Remove the heat source immediately and allow the parts to cool before moving them to a water bath for final cooling. Always wash the piece thoroughly to remove remaining flux which will prevent painting or further adhesives to be used.

As will have been noticed, a little has been said of the advantages of joining a model boat club or society. Joining such an organisation has a lot going for it - there will be many members with experience who will be able to answer queries and may be able to prevent you making any mistakes that they have already made in the past. There will be organised regattas that will bring you into contact with many modellers of similar experience. There will be the pleasure of sailing the model in company with fellow modellers and the enjoyment of participating in the hobby to the full. There will also be the advantage of having the facility of sailing on safe waters with the club's insurance covering any untoward happening to a member of the viewing public. Finally there will be the opportunity of discussing your projects with the experienced members and availing yourself of their advice and help. The social side of the club too can help by drawing other, not necessarily modelling members of the family into the scene where they too can meet others and enjoy sailing days. Under the banner of the Model Power Boat Association most model boat clubs sail in friendly competition with others in the same area to reach an area final from which the best competitors go forward to the National Finals and to gain trophies of real worth. Some of the photographs here illustrate the recent National final competitions.

It should be stressed, however, that not all members of model clubs are highly competitive - many sail for the pure pleasure of it and enjoy the company of fellow modellers of the same feeling. Through the club and the MPBA, however, it is often possible to gain information to cover knotty problems that cannot be solved in any other way, at least not without some serious expense.

Chapter 18   Fishing vessel decks and hatches, radio controls

The forward deck of a large vessel showing the electric windlass, bollards, tank vents etc.

Detail of the fire monitor on the bridge of a large tug.

A few words here about main and shelter decks on fishing vessels. Main and shelter decks are found on merchant ships of various kinds and refer mainly to the location of the deck. Shelter decks are generally the decks found immediately above the main deck of a ship and are so-called because they were originally fitted, only partway from the bow towards the stern, to give shelter to those working on the main deck. On the fishing vessel this is exactly what the shelter deck is for - to protect the crew from the seas breaking over the ship when they are working to the nets etc. Some ships have a shelter deck that extends less than halfway

along the ship from the bow, some have a shelter deck extending three parts of the length of the ship and some are fully shelter-decked.

On the fishing boat there is usually very little machinery on the top of the shelter deck as all the working winches etc., are placed under this deck. Ropes and hawsers needed to work the nets are led through openings in the deck and guided through rollers. The shelter deck will still be fitted with stanchions and rails and upon it will be mounted the mooring bollards, panama fairleads etc. The anchor windlass will, most likely be fitted on this deck forward of the foremast which will be fitted with a derrick or derricks to be used when unloading the catch and, of course, there will be hatches through which access can be gained to the winches, machinery and the fish-rooms below.

Some examples of fishing vessels with full and part shelter decks can be seen in the accompanying photographs and there is a series of sketches illustrating ships with full or part shelter decking. A model of a ship with a full-length or part-length shelter deck need not have a full-length main deck, especially if access to the interior of the model is restricted to small hatches and the main deckhouse. Omitting the forward part of the main deck on such models will reduce weight and allow easier access. However, where an operating anchor system is to be installed or working derricks attached to the foremast, then a sub-deck beneath the shelter deck designed to carry the operating works of the systems is very desirable.

Where working features are to be installed in the model tug or fishing vessel it is wise to plan well ahead and to fit suitable platforms or frames to carry the 'works' i.e. the machinery that controls the operations. As access to such works is vital to the maintenance of equipment, suitable access hatches will be needed and such hatches will need to be as near watertight as possible. The simplest hatch is the one where reasonably high coamings

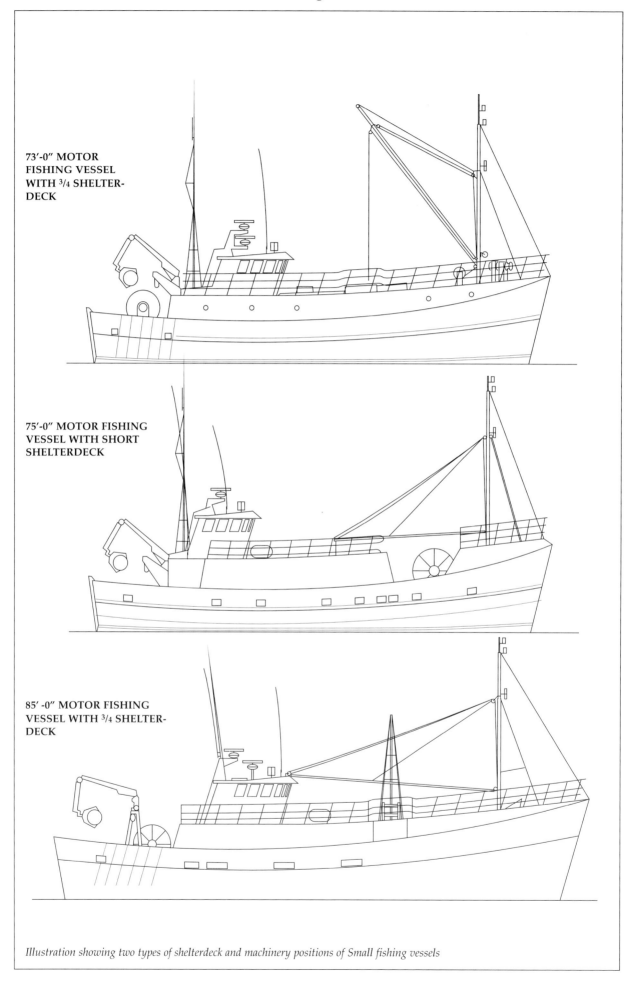

73'-0" MOTOR FISHING VESSEL WITH 3/4 SHELTER-DECK

75'-0" MOTOR FISHING VESSEL WITH SHORT SHELTERDECK

85'-0" MOTOR FISHING VESSEL WITH 3/4 SHELTER-DECK

Illustration showing two types of shelterdeck and machinery positions of Small fishing vessels

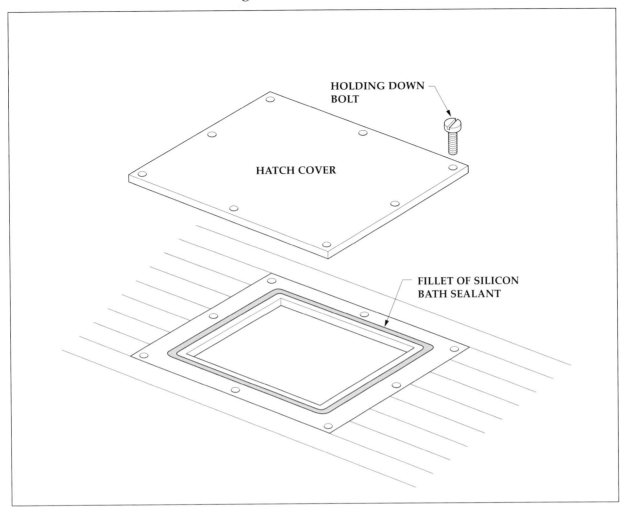

HOLDING DOWN
BOLT

HATCH COVER

FILLET OF SILICON
BATH SEALANT

Method of making a watertight hatch for a model ship

are fitted round the deck opening and the hatch
built up to slip over the coamings neatly and
closely. There will, of course, be places on the
model where raised hatches and coamings cannot
be used and alternative arrangements for access
are needed. If the hatch is fairly high up on a
model running high in the water with little chance
of the deck being flooded frequently then a simple
hatch let into the deck as shown in the sketch here
will be sufficient. Where the hatch is on a deck
that can be flooded regularly then the only answer
is to make a watertight cover fitting flush with the
surrounding deck and using a method of holding
the cover down to its base over a seal such as silicon rubber. A watertight hatch cover system is
also illustrated in the sketches.

Radio control installation

As mentioned earlier, it should always be borne in
mind that electronic and electrical equipment have
an aversion to water, and salt water in particular.
Radio equipment does not take kindly to water at
all and if soaked by accident the equipment
should be dried out as quickly as possible - a hair

dryer is very useful here. If the equipment has
been immersed in salt water then it should be well
rinsed in plenty of clean, fresh water to remove
the salt before being dried. Thus all access points
on the model ship should be given special attention to ensure water cannot enter and harm deli-
cate electronic equipment. Where the model is fitted with steam engine and boiler then the radio
equipment, servos etc., should be isolated from
the steam plant in a compartment from which the
servo rods can be led and rendered steamtight by
means of rubber bellows. Once more, care is
needed and it is sensible to remove all radio
equipment from the steam-powered boat at the
end of each operating session and to store the gear
in a warm dry location until needed again.

More often users of radio equipment fail to locate
their quite expensive equipment correctly in the
model ship. So many modellers know so much
better than the manufacturers don't they? For
example, servos are usually supplied, by the makers, complete with small rubber grommets and
brass ferrules to make up anti-vibration mountings so that the servo is safely installed correctly.

The liferaft canister on a support ship.

Many modellers ignore these facilities and rigidly mount their units with large screws and sometimes with double-sided adhesive tape. If the makers feel that the mountings are needed and take the trouble to supply them then surely it is only wise to use them.

When outfitting the working model tug or trawler seek a suitable location for the radio receiver and its associated battery pack and switch at an early stage in the building programme. Locate the Rx (receiver) in a place remote from the motors to avoid electrical interference with the radio signals

and ensure that the on/off switch for the system is easy accessible. Many modellers make up a radio board or plate that fits neatly into the hull and which can be held in place with two or three brass wood screws to beams fixed across the hull. Such a radio control board can be easily removed when the components need attention or it can be transferred to a second model if need be. The boards illustrated carry, not only the Rx, but the speed controllers and the steering servo too in at least two cases. It is also possible to incorporate into the controls suitable sockets into which the connections from the battery chargers can be plugged to

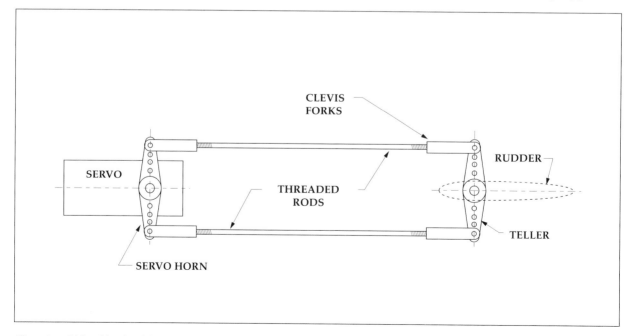

Illstration of 'closed loop' rudder control system using a single servo unit

Liferaft cannister in specially railed off area

charge the batteries without the need to remove them from the model.

In the case of a particularly complex superstructure for a tug or similar model ship, the repeated removal and replacement of the superstructure can result in damage. In this instance it is sensible to consider fitting the on/off switches and charging sockets under a feature on the deck to allow the model to be operated without having the superstructure removed except for attention to motors or controllers etc. A method of carrying out this is shown on the tug *Cruiser* where charging sockets and switches for the radio are hidden under the crate on the starboard side of the engine-room casing; charging sockets and switches for the main drive battery are located under the crate on the port side.

Often one will find that the cable connections of the servo or speed controller will not reach the Rx unit and they need to be altered. Extension cables are available from most model shops to suit the radio equipment that is stocked and it is wise to use such extensions where possible. Those who wish to extend their servo leads using coloured and fine flexible cables can do so by soldering the new cables in to the existing ones and insulating the soldered joints with shrinkwrap tubing. It is also possible to extend the cables using cable connectors of various kinds but be aware that such connectors can create an unacceptable resistance to the current flow. If the cables are extended by soldering in new lengths of wire do be sure that the soldered joint is sound before covering it with

shrinkwrap or other insulation. The use of a small test meter to check the continuity is advised.

Those modellers who wish to use multiple functions to control operating features need to consider the purchase of a multi-channel radio outfit from one of the leading makers. There are units that can be fitted to transmitters which carry a number of switches which, in turn, are repeated in a unit to be mounted in the model and which will switch on lights or small motors etc. when the switch is operated on the transmitter. Sometimes a relay is needed to handle current loads higher than those of the switcher and these are controlled from the switcher. As I am not exactly electronics-literate, I would suggest that the fitting and operation of such switchgear is best left to the expert. In most model clubs you will find someone who is well versed in electronics and/or computer technology and what would we do without them! Some highly skilled modellers fit a form of computer control inside the model which is controlled from the radio and which performs a number of functions, but tugs and trawlers are fairly simple vessels and there is little need for sophisticated controls. A fire monitor or two on a tug, operating lights, towing winch and anchor would just about complete the outfit.

Water pumps

Most working models would benefit from showing the outflow of water from their engine cooling systems - virtually all ships have water discharging from the sides just above the waterline. Such discharges are not difficult to arrange; a small pump is needed and some silicon rubber tubing together with a couple of skin fittings which are small lengths of tube secured firmly to the hull to which pipes can be connected. The pipework needs to be arranged so that the pump draws water from the pond and discharges it through the discharge pipe fitted slightly above the waterline of the ship. One sketch shows how a skin fitting can be made and how to connect the pipes to and from the pump. Note that the skin fittings have a ring round the connection pipe to help hold the rubber pipes securely - it is essential to ensure that the silicon rubber pipes are a very tight fit at each end to prevent water entering the hull and causing subsequent damage or even sinking. As this feature is one that will be operative all the time the model is in the water a simple manual switch is all that is needed.

Radio control

There are other aspects of the radio control equipment to consider, for example, the rudder. In almost all models with few exceptions, the rudder is controlled by the use of a servo. This can be done by connecting a tiller on the top of the rudder stock to a similar servo horn fixed to the servo drive shaft using a hard brass or mild steel rod. The final connections at both ends can be made by simply bending the connecting rod but the best way of effecting this connection is to use clevis forks and threaded rod as shown in the sketches. Such clevises can be bought from most model shops and are used extensively on model aircraft.

Consideration should be given to the size of the rudder and the effect this size will have upon the servo. A fairly large rudder should be connected to the servo using a closed-loop system as illustrated: this provides a balanced push/pull on the servo shaft and puts less strain on the servo motor and its gears. Many models today use steerable Kort nozzles where the nozzle, fitted with a small rudder, rotates round the propeller and steers by guiding the water flow. Here, with a small nozzle, the single rod drive from the servo is acceptable but with most nozzles it is wise to use the closed loop.

Steerable Kort nozzles are of great benefit when a single screw model is running astern when it will be found to steer quite acceptably. Single screw models are notoriously difficult to steer when running astern as, indeed, are full-size single screw ships. To guide a ship backwards with only a single screw demands a great deal of practice and a knowledge of what will happen under differing wind conditions. A good shipmaster will use the

windage of his vessel to aid running astern and this can only be learned in practice.

Bow and stern thrusters

Many tugs and fishing vessels today are fitted with thrusters, usually only at the bow but in larger ships at the stern too. These are available in model form as has been discussed previously and it is quite possible to control a bow or stern thruster from the radio control system. The model sailor will be astonished at the way his/her model performs when a bow thruster is brought into service. Turning in a very short space is so easy and entry to a narrow harbour entrance or to a canal can be accomplished with complete accuracy once you become accustomed to its use. It is very easy to see why the harbour tug has almost disappeared when huge ships such as roll on/roll off (RO/RO) ferries of 30,000 tons can turn and run astern to berth with great accuracy all by themselves under the control of the master on the bridge. A recent visit to a large docks complex revealed a very large bulk carrier ship entering through the lock from the river, it turned within its own length and laid alongside an adjacent quay so slowly and accurately without a tug in sight that I was vastly impressed. With a working bow thruster it is possible to repeat such a manoeuvre with a model and with both bow and stern thrusters it is possible to move a model sideways to a quay very neatly.

Ships' masts

There are some aspects of the model ship that have yet to be dealt with and the first of these is the ship's masts. Virtually all ships have masts, some have only one and others have two or more. The early powered ships carried masts that were also designed to carry sails and to provide power in the event of engine failure. Such masts were usually made of timber, tapering from deck to truck (mast top) and sometimes having a smaller mast fastened to the main section to give additional height. As these masts have disappeared from the maritime scene the emphasis is on the masts of more recent times. Masts are, today, constructed mainly from steel tube and are therefore parallel from the deck to a designed height; sometimes an extension of smaller diameter tube will be used. Despite this type of construction there is a wide variation in mast types as will be seen from the photographs. Some masts carry, not only navigation lights, but also serve as supports for derricks which can be mounted directly on the bottom part of the mast or upon tables attached to the mast base. Some masts serve only to carry radio communication aerials, radar units and other naviga-

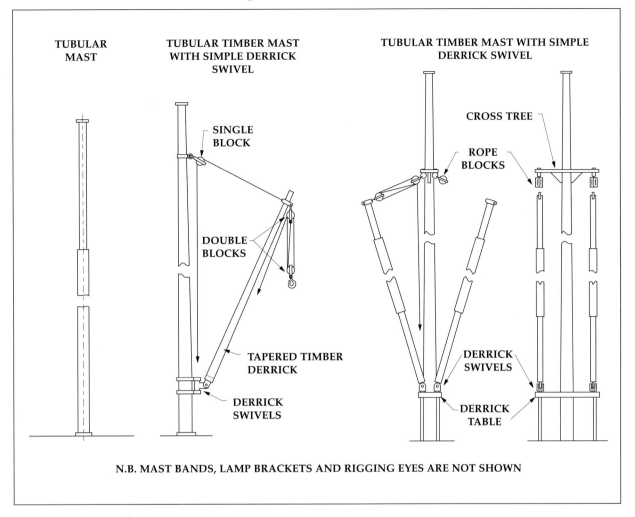

TUBULAR
MAST

TUBULAR TIMBER MAST
WITH SIMPLE DERRICK
SWIVEL

TUBULAR TIMBER MAST WITH SIMPLE
DERRICK SWIVEL

SINGLE
BLOCK

CROSS TREE

ROPE
BLOCKS

DOUBLE
BLOCKS

TAPERED TIMBER
DERRICK

DERRICK
SWIVELS

DERRICK
SWIVELS

DERRICK
TABLE

N.B. MAST BANDS, LAMP BRACKETS AND RIGGING EYES ARE NOT SHOWN

tional direction-finding aerials, while some carry both radio equipment and lighting. There are variations of masts where the design resembles goalposts and where the mast is designed to perform part of the ship's working functions. On some boats, fishing boats in particular, the mast is mounted on top of a gantry which carries cranes or derricks for net handling.

To aid the modeller with mast-making the sketches illustrate some of the mast types recently seen on the modern ship. It will also be noted that some of the very large salvage tugs and pelagic fishing vessels carry cranes of one kind or another in preference to the simple derrick. The modelling of cranes is an exercise in itself although a number of model kit makers list cranes among their ranges of fittings and these small kits can save you many hours of research. Fishing vessels will be found to carry a more diverse range of masting and craneage than can be found on board the tug and you will need to seek data on the derricks and cranes fitted to the chosen vessel so that they can be replicated correctly. For example; the steam-driven tug will almost certainly have at least one small derrick fitted for the specific use of loading coal when, of course, the tug was of the coal-fired type. Steam

tugs and all ships with oil engines will be found to have loading points, usually within small box-like cupboards, for the attachment of flexible pipes when loading fuel oil either from a shore supply or from the bunkering tank ship. You should seek details of such fittings and ensure that they are included on the scale model.

There are other points not previously mentioned in any detail and these refer to such things as lifeboats and liferafts and the provision made for launching them. In the early chapters dealing with *Cruiser* the davits, boats and blocks are fully covered. Many tugs and fishing vessels carried lifeboats under davits of similar types until comparatively recent times. Some types of davits are illustrated in the sketches. The more modern vessels tend to carry a rigid inflatable boat (RIB), or sometimes 2 RIBs, usually under a small crane that can be used for launching and recovery and which is manually operated. Such boats are, in general, constructed of aluminium or timber with an inflatable skirt which makes them virtually unsinkable. In addition the ship will carry at least one and probably two or more liferafts in canisters. When the liferaft canister is opened in an emergency, the liferaft inflates to become an almost totally enclosed boat inside which the occupants can be protected from the elements until they are picked up. Most kit makers and many model shops stock canisters of various sizes which are well made in either white metal or resin. Lifeboats, liferafts and canisters come under the control of the Classification Societies and/or governmental authorities and they must be tested and checked at regular intervals.

You can see that, even when building a kit model, a degree of research into the prototype will be necessary or, at least, some serious discussions with more experienced modellers will be of assistance.

Testing the model

Having installed all the radio equipment and fitted all the features required it is essential that you carry out basin trials. Basin trials are carried out on most newly built ships while the vessel is firmly moored to the fitting-out quay. Engines are run up to full power, electrical installations are fully tested, winches and windlasses are tried etc. The same trials should be carried out on the model before it is taken to the lake for its maiden voyage. As previously mentioned in Chapter 8, the domestic bath is ideal - the garden pond is another possibility provided the goldfish are not upset! Fit all the equipment and have a dry run on the bench first. Then place the model in the bath or pond and test each function. It is possible that the model will ride high in the water and even have a list to port or starboard indicating that ballast must be fitted. Find where the ballast needs to be fitted and carry out ballasting as previously described (Chapter 16) before doing the basin trials. With the model correctly trimmed, try out all the functions one by one, noting any faults or spots where attention is needed. With the help of an assistant check the radio equipment by operating the transmitter at least 100 feet away from the model and seeing the controls respond without problems. Before doing too many further checks, carefully rectify the faults that were obvious in the water. Test the radio equipment again with the transmitter some distance away once more and when all systems operate satisfactorily the model can be prepared for its first outing.

Before going to the lake or pond see that the batteries are fully charged - do not forget that Ni-cads have a memory and need to be fully discharged

before they are charged up. Quickly test the functions and check that shafts etc. have been lubricated, and, finally, make sure that you take spare crystals for the radio in case those fitted clash with another in use at the lake. It is best to choose a day that is calm or has only a light breeze blowing so that there will be no problems trying to test sail in high wave patterns.

The first voyage is always one of keen excitement and anticipation - take a camera to record the event and, above all, watch carefully for little quirky faults that can be remedied later to make safer sailing next time. Do not, of course, take the model to the lake if the paint was only applied the night before. If it hasn't had time to dry properly you will have problems with the paint finish later - most paint finishes need at least three weeks to permit the volatiles contained therein to evaporate and the surface to harden fully.

Allow only 15 to 20 minutes sailing for the first session and bring the model in so that the motor can be tested for heat, the propeller(s) checked for security and freedom of weed and all the internals examined for water contamination. Look carefully into the bottom of the hull to see if there is any water build up; when running astern it is not unusual to ship a little water up the shaft(s) particularly if there is some end play. Such end play can be rectified in the workshop but always be sure that the shaft is free to turn after making such adjustments. If all appears in order then a second short sailing session is in order. Short sessions with examination checks in between should be the order of the day on the maiden trip to the lake. Model boating is to be enjoyed and there is much to be learned when sailing a new model before you can be said to be a proficient sailor. Over the next few sessions you will learn of the model's quirks - all models have them, even if built from the same plans two models will perform differently. A good modeller will spend time learning his model's performance so that eventually he/she will sail the ship with complete confidence.

Only by being fully aware of the model's performance will the competitive sailor be able to enter and win local, regional and, who knows, national regattas. It is useless to try winning if the model behaves in an unexpected way each time it is brought out.

Chapter 19   Painting and tools

A mast with navigation lights

The finishing of the model ship, while briefly dealt with previously, is one which needs to be done most carefully, particularly if the model is to be entered into competition or placed upon display for inspection by the general public. We have all, no doubt, seen the beautiful models produced by ship-builders for their clients in previous years and currently on display in some of the maritime museums. These magnificent models once graced the offices of the large shipowners who, sadly today, no longer exist. It was rare for a shipowner not to be provided with a shipbuilder's model once an order was in hand for a number of similar ships.

It may seem that such high standards cannot be reached in the working model but this is not the case today. Thirty or so years ago the working ship model was quite crude by today's standards; the fittings available from the few makers of the day were also crude and heavy. No-one thought that a museum-quality model could be sailed safely due mainly to the heavy weights of the materials available then. Hulls of glass fibre and resin were not available nor were finely cast fittings in lightweight resin or white metal. Radio control equipment was unreliable, bulky and very expensive and electric motors were much different to those of today. There was little difference in steam plants except that they had to be built by the modeller and few were available for purchase from the model shop.

It goes without saying that the early modellers had, most of the time, to be very ingenious and be prepared to make very nearly everything that was to be fitted. Today there is a wealth of fittings available at very reasonable prices and high quality radio control equipment can be bought for modest sums. Electric motors in a large range of sizes and prices can be seen in most of the bigger model shops and fully completed and working steam plants can be found at fair prices from specialist makers. Fine working model ships can be bought in kit form where, in some cases, there is little more work needed than the assembly of numbered parts using the adhesives and methods described in the instruction manuals. The quality of models built from kits today rivals the quality of models that can be produced by the expert modeller working from scratch. There is really no reason why models of a quality close to that of the museum models cannot be built by the hobby modeller prepared to work sensibly and diligently today.

First let us look at the quality of paintwork and the brushes required. Like tools, brushes need to be bought with care. The fine brushes used by the watercolour artist are excellent for applying paint to the model, particularly acrylic paint where the brushes can be washed in water and left to dry. The very best, and the most expensive, are those carrying the label Kolinsky Sable - they come in a range of sizes from 000 to 12 all with points and from 1/4in. to 1in. as flats. Always clean the brush after it has been used, in thinners for oil paint, and wash it well before standing it, head up, in a jar to dry. Try to keep each brush for a specific colour as this will prevent paint carry over from one colour to another; some paint will stay in the bristles occasionally even if the brush is well washed. Do not use the fine sable brushes for dusting or other tasks that will allow the heads to become dirty. When it comes to power painting then an airbrush is possibly the best buy for fine work. Cans of airbrush propellant are not expensive but a small air compressor and container tank will give better and more consistent pressure at the airbrush. As is the case with brushes, the airbrush needs to be kept clean and well serviced after use. Jars of paint can be mixed and kept for some time if well sealed. It is usual to thin the paint with 50% of thinners, designed for fast drying times, and, to avoid poor paint matching, it is sensible to mix sufficient paint to do the whole job before starting to spray.

Most car accessory shops stock a range of colours for cars that come in both cellulose, synthetic and acrylic forms some of which, in particular the primers, are ideal for use by the modeller for painting hulls etc. The most popular paint seems to be that made by Humbrol and sold in most model shops; the greatest colour range is in small tinlets with a smaller range in slightly larger tins. There are some colours available in spray cans and there is a range of matt, satin and gloss varnish too. A growing range of acrylic paint is being marketed by Humbrol and a number of other makers in the UK and there is little doubt that similar ranges are produced in other countries including the USA. When brush painting with either enamels or acrylics it is wise to thin the medium and to apply a number of thin coats in preference to a single heavy coat, the finish will be much better. Applying two or three coats of clear varnish will protect the model from fingermarks especially if the model is in a matt finish. Matt paints tend to show fingermarks very easily and clear, matt varnish will prevent this.

There are no shortcuts to achieving a fine paint finish to the model. As mentioned earlier, preparation is all-important - smooth paintwork can only be achieved over a smooth surface. The good modeller will pay particular attention to the surfaces to which paint is to be applied and prepare

My Badger 200 airbrush used for painting much of the small detail parts and surfaces.

A small air compressor which is invaluable for use with an airbrush obviating the need for frequent stops when using a canned propellant.

the surface carefully. Every blemish must be rectified, holes and hollows must be filled and the whole area coated with a good quality primer. At least three coats of primer are advisable whether applied from a spray can, an airbrush or by hand brushing. Each coat should be allowed to dry properly before the next is applied and the surface area should be examined between each coat so that any faults that become apparent may be rubbed down and rectified. The finish paint whether it be gloss, satin or matt finish should be mixed carefully and thinned where necessary. Once more at least three coats will be needed for a good finish and each coat will need to be lightly rubbed down when it is dry and before the next coat is applied. Bear in mind always that paint, while touch-dry in an hour or so, will not be fully hard and resistant to wear and knocks for as long as three weeks in normal conditions. This period can be shortened by keeping the model in a warm and dry atmosphere for about 7 days. When using the modern car paint spray cans be aware that these finishes are designed for hardening in a conditioned paint booth where the temperature of the booth, once the car has been painted, is raised to around 160 degrees Fahrenheit and the car held

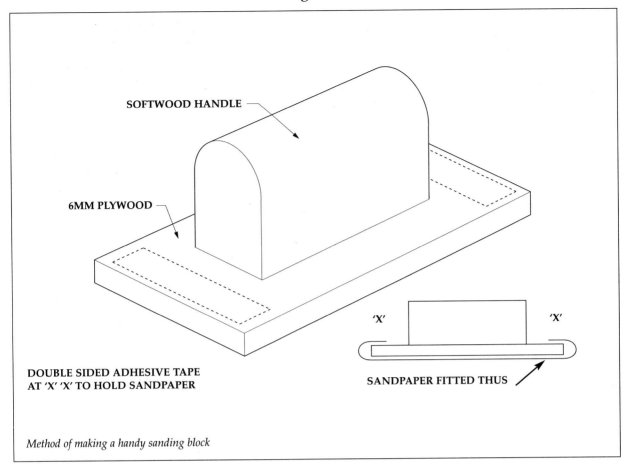

SOFTWOOD HANDLE

6MM PLYWOOD

DOUBLE SIDED ADHESIVE TAPE
AT 'X' 'X' TO HOLD SANDPAPER

'X'   'X'

SANDPAPER FITTED THUS

Method of making a handy sanding block

therein for some 40 minutes. The model, once painted, should be set aside to allow the paint to dry out properly. If the hull has been painted then it will be possible to proceed with work on superstructures etc. in the interim.

It is important too to finish the model correctly using a matt varnish. Ships do not appear glossy and shiny even when newly painted, at best they can be said to be in a satin finish. If the model is to be used regularly and entered in competitions involving sailing as well as being judged out of the water then it is wise to finish it in a matt varnish as this will show best to the judges and other observers. If, however, the model is to be built for display within a glass case or similar enclosure then, quite often, a satin or semi-matt finish will show it off better.

Chapter 1 briefly mentioned the tools required for building model ships. A good craft knife is a must - one with snap-off blade sections is most probably the best as it gives you access to new and keen points whenever the first becomes blunt or broken. This tool used with a good steel straightedge will readily cut thin plywood up to 2.0mm and score or cut styrene of thicknesses up to 4.0mm. It will also be of use for cutting card and thin stripwood and for cutting and trimming balsa and jelutong. Such knives can be found in most good DIY outlets, in craft, in some model shops and in

good tool stores. Coupled with the craft knife is the steel rule or straightedge and you should seek one of stainless steel, preferably 12in. long with metric and imperial scales. This will serve not only to measure and mark the work for cutting or preparation but also to guide the craft knife when cutting - it is almost impossible to cut straight lines freehand. Such rules can be bought in the same outlets as the craft knife.

For accurate marking an engineer's steel square is of great value; these come in sizes from 3in. to 6in. and in mild or stainless steel. The mild steel is quite adequate and the 4in. size is a good buy. A self-sealing cutting mat is of great value - it will save its value in knife blades in a short while and provide a non-slip surface upon which to cut all manner of material. Cutting mats can be found in many shops particularly those dealing with artist's materials and some of the larger tool stores and stationers.

For the kit builder very little more will be needed save, perhaps, a fine tenon saw for cutting the thicker plywoods and stripwood and a selection of small drill bits and a hand drill. A good sanding block is an asset and the accompanying sketch illustrates a suitable sanding block - almost all sanding should be done using a block in preference to holding the abrasive paper in the hand. For wet-and-dry paper used wet, a hard rubber block is ideal.

Some of the tools used by me for model making.

For the more advanced modeller there are a number of small tools that will be of value, especially if the ship model is to be built from scratch. There are mail order companies who specialise in tools and workshop equipment and many of these take stand space at the exhibitions held in various parts of the country. A visit to such outlets is frequently well worthwhile as quality tools are sometimes offered at quite low prices. One or two small drill holders for hand drilling using very fine drills are a useful purchase. A selection of small screwdrivers of the three types of point are also handy particularly when working on the electrics of the model. A pair of small fine jaw pliers and a pair of side cutting pliers will also be of value. The larger domestic type of plier and screwdriver, while useful, will probably be too big for most modelling jobs. A fretsaw is a valuable addition to the tool kit where a reasonable amount of cutting is needed and where the cutting is in curves. This will require a cutting table which is small and clamps to the edge of the bench. If a real investment is contemplated then a mains-operated vibro-type fretsaw is of great value. I have one that has been in use for more than 20 years and it is an invaluable tool. The cost of such a tool is, of course, very high and could not be justified unless a great deal of work is to be done. One advantage of the fretsaw is the ability to fit blades that will cut metal in place of the wood-cutting ones and this means that small pieces of brass and copper are easily dealt with when needed.

The modeller building ships by the plank-on-frame method will need a good pin hammer; one and a half to two ounces in weight is ideal for driving small pins when planking a hull. Such hammers can be found at all good tool stores but less easily from the larger DIY outlets. One which has a ball pein-type head is best. The head that drives the pins or nails should be kept clean and polished - heads contaminated with glue or other dirt cause nails and pins to bend more easily than a polished head. This may sound strange but it is a fact that a hammer with a dirty head will slip more easily than a clean one.

A very useful tool for the modeller's workshop is the small low-voltage mini-drill, often sold in a package containing a number of drills, burrs, stones and even a small circular saw blade and polishing mop. Usually suitable for running from a 12-volt supply fed through a transformer from the mains, such drills have many uses as they are easily hand held and they are light. There are a number of accessories available such as a bench stand, lathe attachment, router etc. which turn the drill outfit into an almost complete engineering workshop. These drills and outfits can vary enormously in price so it is wise to investigate all aspects of the system before buying.

Before leaving hand tools altogether, consideration must be given to wood chisels which are of great use when carving the bow and stern blocks of a model in timber but also useful for other tasks such as cutting window apertures from styrene sheet. If the corners of the windows are first drilled to give the required corner curve then a sharp chisel pressed firmly down on the window line will cleanly cut through styrene up to 1.5mm thick purely by the pressure imposed.

This is much easier and more accurate than cutting between the corners with a craft knife. Another useful tool from the cabinetmaker's craft is the spokeshave which is very handy for shaping curves in timber; two types of spokeshave can be found but the standard unit used for smoothing the outsides of curves is likely to be the most useful.

Moving into the power tool range there is little use for a power screwdriver unless you are going to build display cabinets and the like, but a power-driven sander is superb for removing excess timber and rendering the outer surface of a hull smooth enough for priming coats of paint. A pedestal drill is an item which has much to recommend it but again one must weigh the cost against the work it will do and the time that can be saved to justify high prices. The lathe, whether it be for wood turning or a metal-working unit, is an item of high cost and yet very useful to the modeller with workshop space and a genuine use to place against its cost. For example, I invested in my first lathe only days before this chapter was written having managed successfully for over 25 years without one. It must be said that it is now in almost daily use and will very rapidly pay for itself in time saved and better quality work, but this is in a professional's workshop and it must not be confused with the needs of the hobbyist.

Many electrical tool makers offer powered files, circular saws, bandsaws and other fairly large power tools designed to cut wood of varying thicknesses and to save time and this is all well and good if the cost can be justified. If, for instance, you are a keen DIY person and have a use for power tools round the house then the fact that they are there will save time when modelling. The novice shipbuilder has no real need for power tools and very high-class models can be built using small hand tools alone. The best way to build up a good tool kit is to buy a given tool when a need is felt, to buy only the very best that can be found and to learn to take good care of the tool once it is purchased. It is the bad worker who blames the tools and it is sensible for the novice to learn how to use and care for his/her tools properly - if necessary by attending a class run by the local college or local authority.

When you come to installing radio control equipment and electrics then a good electric soldering iron is a must. For electronic work an iron rated at 15 or up to 25 watts is recommended but when soldering heavy cables to speed boards such as Bob's boards then a bigger iron will be needed rated at 75 or 100 watts. The latter large irons could form part of the domestic toolkit in many homes. How to use such soldering equipment has already been described. For free soldering or silver soldering a small blowlamp is a must and the range of these available is quite vast. It is wise to discuss your requirements with the shop selling blowlamps or with a knowledgeable colleague at the local boat club.

Chapter 20 Care of the model and shell plating notes

Having completed the model ship it is sensible to examine it carefully to ensure that nothing has been missed or omitted, and also to check that there are no areas that need to be trimmed and/or touched up with paint and varnish. The most sensible way to tackle the final examination is by preparing a checklist and, by using this, to go over the entire model. A good checklist can be prepared from the General Arrangement drawings. Start at the bows and list every item shown on the drawings, both in the plan view and in the profile. Compare the list with photographs until it details even the smallest part or place on the ship. Set the model up on its stand and then proceed to check the model against the list, item by item. It is a good idea to have a friend or colleague to assist

with this as, quite often, you will miss an item that has been missed before.

As previously mentioned, dust is the biggest problem that next faces the modeller and Chapter 9 gives details on how to construct a carry case for your model.

Often, at the lakeside, there will be a number of spectators showing interest in the models and enjoying the spectacle of the ships on the water. It is difficult to prevent people and particularly children from touching the models but it is also a shame to prevent them from seeing the ship model out of the water. This situation can be remedied by making the carry case into a display

A carry/display case for a working model of the Rix Harrier. Note the space left for storage of the R/C equipment (built by the author).

case too. Many of the large DIY outlets stock clear polystyrene sheet of about 3 or 4mm thickness for use in making greenhouses and other garden articles. This material can be used easily to replace one of the sides of the carry case and thus permit the model to be displayed without anyone being able to touch it. Little boys especially love models that work and they will spend hours looking and learning - they seem to have eyes on the ends of their fingers as they have the need to touch everything they see. Many model boat clubs have a few model ships of one kind or another made specifically for youngsters to try their hands at sailing and this is an excellent way to draw the young folk into the club. Many clubs also have evenings in the winter time when instruction is provided for those novice and junior modellers wishing to learn the finer points of ship building. The demise of the shipbuilding industry in the UK has shut down the apprentice schools where so many learned their craft - shipbuilder's models were often produced in the apprentice training schools of the big shipyards and many of the modellers of today worked on such models in their youth.

Some modellers prefer to build static models and throughout the world there are many who build very fine static model ships. Within the international competition system under the control of NAVIGA, the ruling body for the model ship hobby, there is a section devoted specifically to the static model and part of class 'C'. 'C' class championships are held regularly both in the UK and abroad and the quality of workmanship is extremely high. Virtually all these models are fitted into cabinets made from glass and timber or, sometimes, polycarbonate is used instead of glass. There are specialist companies who will supply purpose-built cabinets for display purposes but it is not outside the scope of the average modeller to produce a suitable display case as outlined in Chapter 9.

Once the carry or display case has been built and the model has been examined for faults and been put into good order it will need to be cleaned before placing it in its case. There are a number of very small and battery driven vacuum cleaners to be found mostly in computer stores - these cleaners are ideal for reaching into awkward corners or places and removing fine dust. The hull of the model can be lightly cleaned with warm water and detergent and dried with a soft cloth, parts of the superstructure will also benefit from a light wash. Take great care, however, and be very wary of using proprietary cleaners which can damage the paint finish or leave an unsightly smear. Obviously this degree of work is not necessary for the model that is to spend most of the season sailing on the local lake or pond, but it is a good idea

The completed model of Academus *in its timber and glass display case.*

A completed static model of Rix Harrier *on the base of its display case.*

to do this cleaning at the end of the sailing season so that the model is stored in a clean condition.

Storing the working model, even for short periods, needs attention. Radio receivers and batteries are best removed from the model and kept in a cool, dry place. Nicad batteries should be fully discharged and stored in the discharged state. Lead-acid type batteries should be cleaned thoroughly externally, and, in contrast to nicads, charged up fully and then placed in a cool, dry place. Under no circumstances should you allow the radio gear and batteries to be placed in a situation where they can be frozen or frosted as this will cause serious and, possibly, irreparable damage. The model itself should be stored in similar conditions and should be dry both inside and out before storage.

The propeller shaft(s) will benefit from being cleaned of old lubricant and re-greased before storing and other working parts should be cleaned and cared for prior to storage.

When visiting the regatta scene at the various locations round the country you will be surprised

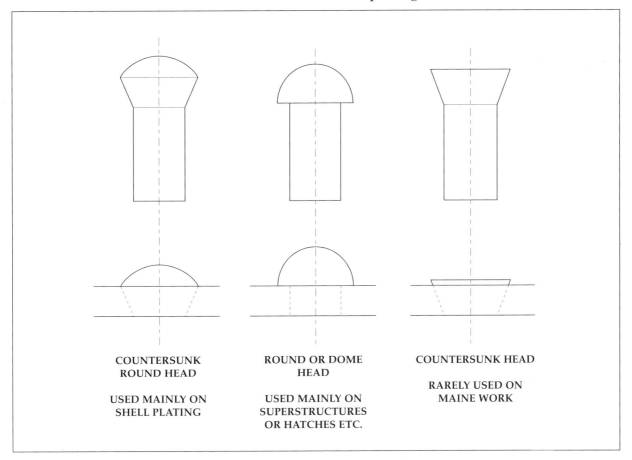

COUNTERSUNK
ROUND HEAD

USED MAINLY ON
SHELL PLATING

ROUND OR DOME
HEAD

USED MAINLY ON
SUPERSTRUCTURES
OR HATCHES ETC.

COUNTERSUNK HEAD

RARELY USED ON
MAINE WORK

to see the same models appear year after year. This would not be possible if the models were not treated with care and stored carefully over the winter months. Some model boaters do sail in the winter, of course, and it is not unknown for the hardy one to break the ice on the lake in order to allow him/her to sail a model. One or two builders have even constructed model icebreakers and tried them out on the thin ice of the lake - regretfully there seems to be no notes of their successes or failures in this venture. Icebreaking tugs are used in certain areas of Europe to break ice in rivers and canals to ensure that commercial traffic can continue and it is possible that such a model tug, correctly weighted and ballasted, could perform a similar task in good conditions and on very thin ice. Whether you would wish to see many months of painstaking work subjected to the rigours of icebreaking is another matter.

As previously mentioned, in the UK the model boat fraternity is catered for under the auspices of the Model Power Boat Association (MPBA) and the section of this association that deals with scale models is the Scale Section (see Appendix 2 for details). Almost all model boat clubs are affiliated to the MPBA and run their competitions and events under the guidance of the association. As has been stated more than once before, membership of a model boat club has many advantages, not the least being access to a lake or pond that has been examined and is suitable for model boat sailing or has been built specifically for model boats. In addition the club will carry public liability insurance cover which will safeguard the modeller relative to the general public.

The model press (see Appendix 2) should not be overlooked. The monthly and quarterly journals give details of how models are built by others, provide advice on aspects of ship model building and review new products and kits. Most journals also have a division that produces plans and sometimes ship model hulls, at quite modest prices. Such plans are also usually catalogued by the degree of difficulty in building a model from them so that the novice will not buy the plans of a complex warship without knowing in advance that it will be very difficult to construct. These magazines are a source of much information and the editorial staff are usually skilled model shipbuilders specialising one type of ship or another. All the staff of these journals are invariably helpful and friendly and assist the newcomer particularly by pointing him/her in the direction needed for the advice that is sought. As also previously mentioned, maritime museums are also a good source of data and information.

Models can be built from photographs but, unless the builder has experience, this is a particularly difficult thing to do. Even after many years of model shipbuilding the thought of having to build purely from photographs is a daunting even to me. There is one saving grace in this instance - ships very often have the same hull form even when of different sizes so that it is sometimes possible to use an existing drawing to aid the construction of a hull. It will be obvious by now that the easiest entry into model shipbuilding, as far as the novice is concerned, is the small kit produced by the specialist manufacturer. The more experienced modeller will seek the larger and more complex kit or graduate to building models from scratch as this will give more individuality to his/her models.

Finally a few points to remember and bear in mind when building the model ship, whether it be from a kit or from scratch. Ships built before World War 2 were almost invariably of steel with riveted construction which was the norm in those days. Many wartime ships combined riveting with welding and were thus a mixture. Ships built after World War 2 became increasingly totally welded until the riveted joints disappeared and the familiar sound of riveting disappeared from the yards. Be particularly careful about applying rivets to a model they are best omitted if they cannot be shown correctly. There are a number of ways of showing rivets all of which have been described in the model press over the years but not always in a realistic manner. Rivets used to fix hull plating to the frames of ships and to each other were invariably of the type known as countersunk round heads shown in the accompanying sketches. This type of rivet is almost invisible from a short distance, especially when the hull of the ship has had a few coats of paint -only the dome projects and this by only a short way. The more obvious rivet detail is generally found on the superstructures and decks of ships where dome headed rivets were used.

The countersunk rivet on shell plating was used to provide a tighter joint and assist in rendering the shell watertight, whereas the round head or dome head rivets were used elsewhere. Obviously there is more work involved providing countersunk holes in the plating than in just plain drilling and costs could be saved by using dome headed rivets where the joints did not justify such tightness. The plates too, were overlapped for riveting or there would be a butt plate used to allow the ends of the plates to be butted together. Such butts would indicate the rivet lines and frequency. The intervals between rivets and the number of rows of rivets were and are laid down by the Classification Societies and it is necessary for the purist modeller to research this relative to his/her chosen ship.

Welded construction of ships is the norm today and it is rare to find a ship built with overlapping platework and welded joints. Plates today are profile cut on special welding and cutting machines in many cases and then welded edge-to-edge over the hull frames. Quite often the holes and flanges for the attachment of bilge pipes and other skin fittings are fitted to the plates before they are welded to the ship and, of course, computer control of many welding and cutting tasks is becoming more frequent. The smooth lines of the hull of the ship of riveted construction have also gone and are now replaced by the unsightly wavy lines of the welded hull. Looking along the lines of a welded ship, the plates will be found to be slightly distorted and this phenomenon is caused by the heat of the welding setting up an uneven expansion and contraction of individual plates. This does not occur in the riveted hull as the plates were not subjected to heat as they were fixed in place - only the rivets were red hot and only one at a time thus causing almost no stress.

Small items that need to be looked at carefully are such things as fairleads, bollards, tank vents and other small fittings found on and round the decks of the ship. All come under the inspection and testing of the Classification Society's surveyors and almost all can be found in tables in some of the many marine books published over the years. The staff at Lloyds Register of Ships are usually very considerate and helpful when information is requested of them and there is little doubt that the other Societies such as Bureau Veritas will also assist. Many of their surveyors have offices at the large ports and dock areas where polite enquiries can be addressed.

Radio frequencies have been briefly mentioned but it is important to know and remember that only specific bands within the 27 Mhz and 40 Mhz ranges apply to model boats. It is illegal to operate a model boat radio system outside these bands - 35 Mhz for example is restricted to model aircraft. These are the wavebands applicable in the UK. Other countries have different wavebands, if you are taking a model abroad then it is sensible to check that the radio system complies with the local regulations. All model boat clubs have data on these regulations and can assist the newcomer. Not all model shops are quite so well informed, so that the model shop specialising in model ships is the informed source as a rule. There are a number of channels within each radio band to which the R/C outfit can be tuned by means of crystals and no two models sporting the same crystals in the same band may sail at the same time as serious interference will result. The chances of Citizens' Band radio causing interference with model boat outfits is now quite rare but does happen on odd occasions.

Much has been written about radio control of models and there are many informed sources available to the modeller mainly through books and extra curricular education classes. The novice modeller will gain help and information from the model club and its members much more easily.

The hobby of model ship building and sailing is one that can provide a great deal of pleasure to young and old alike. The properly built and ballasted model will sail beautifully and rarely sink except in exceptional circumstances in contrast to the fine model aircraft that may crash land on its first outing and be virtually destroyed.

Furthermore it is a hobby that is enjoyed in the fresh air which benefits the owner in contrast to the general run of model railways which are indoor activities. No hobby is without cost and some are very much more expensive than others. In this respect the model ship hobby is no worse than others. A great deal of money can be spent on high quality model ship kits, if you so wish, but it is also possible to build a fine ship model on a very tight budget indeed.

I have been building model ships, both powered and static types, for many years and even though it is a full-time occupation it is still a pleasure and a joy to see the finished project after some months of work.

Happy modelling!

Appendix 1
Kit Manufacturers

Caldercraft:
Jotika Ltd.
Unit 7
Highgrove Farm
Pinvin
WorcsWR10 2LF

Deans Marine
Conquest Drove
Farcet Fen
Peterborough PE7 3DH

Graupner
Ripmax Ltd. (importer)
Ripmax Corner
Green Street
Enfield EN3 7SJ

Lesro Ltd.
Stony Lane
Christchurch
Dorset BH23 7LQ

The Model Slipway
77 Arundell Drive
Lundwood
Barnsley S71 5LE

Mount Fleet Models
Laurel Mount
79 Holmfirth Road
Meltham
Huddersfield HD7 3DA

Robbe Schluter UK
Unit 53
Hinckley Workspace
Southfield Road
Hinckley
Leicester LE10 2AS

R M Marine
Chester House
The Dingle
Colwyn Bay
North Wales

Semi-Kits

The following supply hulls with drawings or semi-kits comprising hull, drawings and some fittings.

Kingston Mouldings
411 Ringwood Road
Parkstone
Poole
Dorset BH12 4LX

Mouldeans
Conquest Drove
Farcet Fen
Peterborough PE7 3DH

Sirmar
Unit 48
Meadow Mills
Dixon Street
Kidderminster DY10 1HH

Note: The above makers all carry tugs and/or fishing boats within their range of ship kits.
The following European manufacturers may have tug and fishing boats in their ranges and such kits can be found at most good model shops:
Aeronaut
Amati
Artesania Latina
Billings
Corel
Krick
Mantua
Panart
Sergal

Dumas kits imported from the USA have at least one tug in their range and some American fishing vessels.

Appendix 2

Plans Services

Brown Son & Ferguson Ltd.
4-10 Darnley Street
Glasgow G41 2SD

David Macgregor Plans
12 Upper Oldfield Park
Bath BA2 3JZ

Jecobin
31 Romans Way
Pyrford
Woking
Surrey GU22 8TR

Marine Modelling International
Traplet Publications Ltd.
Traplet House
Severn Drive
Upton-upon-Severn
Worcs WR8 0JL

Model Boats Plans Service
Nexus Special Interests Ltd.
Nexus House
Azalea Drive
Swanley
Kent BR8 8HU

Model Shipwright Plans
Maritime Models
7 Nelson Road
Greenwich
London SE10 9JR
Tel: 0181 858 5661

Taubman Plans Service International
11 College Drive
Jersey City
New Jersey 07305
USA

Shops specialising in Marine Modelling and Mail Order

Derby Marine Models
16 George Street
Derby DE1 1EH
Tel: 01332 202706

Maritime Models
7 Nelson Road
Greenwich
London SE 10 9JR
Tel: 0181 858 5661

Midway Models
157 St Leonards Road
Leicester LE2 3BZ
Tel: 0116 270 1609

The Model Dockyard (mail order only)
17 Tremorvah Barton
Tregolls Road
Truro
Cornwall TR1 1NN
Tel: 01872 222120

E Radestock
2 Government Road
Hoylake
Wirral
Merseyside L47 2DB
Tel: 0151 632 1566

Squires Model & Craft Tools
100 London Road
Bognor Regis
West Sussex PO21 1DD
41 Seamoor Road
Westbourne
Bournemouth
BH4 9AE
Tel: 01202 763480

Suppliers of Specialist Equipment

Steam outfits
Cheddar Models Ltd.
Sharpham Road
Cheddar
Somerset BS27 3DR

John Burrell Engineers Ltd
The Steam Gallery
Thorganby
North Yorks

R M Marine
Chester House
The Dingle
Colwyn Bay
North Wales

Stour Valley Steam Engines
Applecroft
Watery Lane
Pillerton Hersey
Warwick CV35 0QP

Trylon Ltd.
Wollaston
Northants
NN29 7QJ

Unit Steam Engines (USE)
The Coach House
Rose Cottage
London Road
Mickleham
Surrey RH5 6EH

Flags and pennants
Little Models
Mike Allsop
23 Hebden Walk
Grantham
Lincs NG31 9TU

Model ship fittings
James Lane (Display Models)
30 The Broadway
Blyth
Northumberland NE24 2PP

Precision Controls
3 Chantry Avenue
Bideford
Devon EX39 2QW

Quay Craft
Harbour Cottage
2 Quayfield Road
Ilfracombe
Devon EX34 9EN

E Radestock
2 Government Road
Hoylake
Wirral
Merseyside L47 2DB
Tel: 0151 632 1566

Propellers and shafts
The Prop Shop
Unit 5
Alscot Park Stables
Preston-on-Stour
Warwickshire CV37 8BL

E Radestock
2 Government Road
Hoylake
Wirral
Merseyside L47 2DB

Electronic controls Action
140 Holme Court Avenue
Biggleswade
Beds SG18 9PB

Electronise Design
2 Hillside Road
Four Oaks
Sutton Coldfield B74 4DQ

Fleet Control Systems
47 Fleet Road
Fleet
Hampshire GU13 8PJ

Hunter Systems
24 Aspen Road
Eastbourne
East Sussex BN22 0TG

Model Boating Organisations

Model Power Boat Association (MPBA)
Mrs J Garner (General Secretary)
5 Fox Close
Boston
Lincs PE21 8EE

Magazines

Marine Modelling International (monthly)
Traplet Publications Ltd.
Traplet House
Severn Drive
Upton-upon-Severn
Worcs WR8 0JL

Model Boats (monthly)
Nexus Special Interests Ltd.
Nexus House
Azalea Drive
Swanley
Kent BR8 8HU

Model Shipwright (quarterly)
Conway Maritime Press
33 John Street
London WC1N 2AT

Sea Breezes
202 Cotton Exchange Building
Old Hall Street
Liverpool L3 0LA

Ships Monthly
22 Branston Road
Burton-on-Trent DE14 3BT

Seaways Publishing Inc.
2271 Constitution Drive
San Jose
California 95124
USA

Appendix 3

Methods of preparing camber curves

Many ships today are built without sheer or camber curves and the sketch below illustrates a straight line camber where the centre part of the deck is level for a short way. The sketch shows the graphic method of setting up the camber.

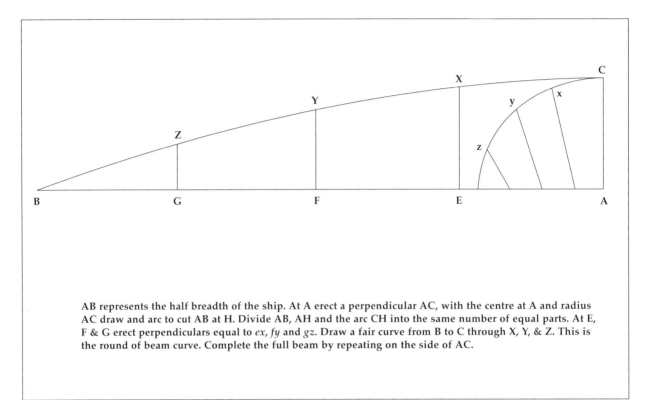

AB represents the half breadth of the ship. At A erect a perpendicular AC, with the centre at A and radius AC draw and arc to cut AB at H. Divide AB, AH and the arc CH into the same number of equal parts. At E, F & G erect perpendiculars equal to *ex*, *fy* and *gz*. Draw a fair curve from B to C through X, Y, & Z. This is the round of beam curve. Complete the full beam by repeating on the side of AC.